Southern Illinois University Press
Carbondale and Edwardsville

The IQ Mythology

Class, Race, Gender, and Inequality

Elaine Mensh and
Harry Mensh

Library of Congress Cataloging-in-Publication Data

Mensh, Elaine
    The IQ mythology: class, race, gender, and inequality / Elaine
Mensh and Harry Mensh.
        p.   cm.
    Includes bibliographical references and index.
    1. Intelligence tests.   2. Test bias.   3. Intelligence levels—
Social aspects.   4. Educational tests and measurements.
I. Mensh, Harry.   II. Title.
BF432.A1M46   1991
153.9′3—dc20   90-37475
ISBN 0-8093-1666-8   CIP

The paper used in this publication meets the minimum requirements of
American National Standard for Information Sciences—Permanence
of Paper for Printed Library Materials, ANSI Z39.48-1984. ⊚

The questions which one asks oneself begin, at last, to illuminate the world, and become one's key to the experience of others. One can only face in others what one can face in oneself. On this confrontation depends the measure of our wisdom and compassion.

—James Baldwin, *Nobody Knows My Name*

Contents

Acknowledgments

Our thanks to Curtis L. Clark, our editor, whose acuity, judgment, and concern we value. James D. Simmons, Susan H. Wilson, and Natalia Nadraga also contributed to the kind of publishing experience writers hope for. And thanks also to copyeditors John Killheffer and Mara Lou Hawse.

Introduction

How deeply IQ tests, or the mythology surrounding them, have entered the national consciousness is evident from the virtually standard use of "IQ" as a synonym for "intelligence." But there are many other striking expressions of this phenomenon, including the way the tests turn up in works of fiction.

"[T]here was the idiotic testimony of those peculiar witnesses, IQ tests: those scores invented me," observes the narrator in a well-known book of autobiographical short stories. "Those scores were a decisive piece of destiny in that they affected the way people treated you and regarded you; they determined your authority."[1] The narrator is unusual; he has reason to be pleased with the way IQ scores invented him, yet he assures his readers that the invention is based on "idiotic testimony."

Although IQ scores invented the narrator/author, the invention was not haphazard or accidental; it took place along well-established guidelines or, more accurately, class and racial lines. The narrator is middle-class. He is white. His (adoptive) parents, who were born before the last century ended, probably completed their education during World War I. At a time when high school was reserved for a small part of the population, both parents graduated from high school; the mother went on to two years of college.

The narrator/author grew up in Missouri in the thirties and early forties. He belonged to a Boy Scout troop that was exclusively middle- and upper-middle-class. One boy hummed Brahms, another knew some of Shakespeare's plays by heart. IQ tests do not call for a real interest in culture, but they do require an acquaintance with selected aspects of the dominant culture (one IQ test literally calls for a recognition of Shakespearean characters, another for knowing the instruments in a symphony orchestra).

At the school the narrator attended, "the varying kinds of

middle-class children, the few rich, and the slightly more nu-merous poor met."[2] They met, however briefly, but their IQ scores did not; the tests that invented middle- and upper-middle-class children in one way invented poor children in another. The scores also invented black children, who were attending their separate and unequal schools. Or, to be precise, the scores gave "scientific" credibility to pre-existing inventions of African-American children in particular but also of poor white ones as inferior in intelligence, and of middle- and upper-middle-class white children as superior in intelligence.

The narrator's observation that IQ-test scores "affected the way people treated you and regarded you" is not simply the impressionistic reaction of an imaginative individual. On the contrary, the scores' influence on the way teachers treat chil-dren—known as the "Pygmalion effect"—has been well docu-mented. In a classic experiment, teachers were told that IQ tests had shown certain children to be "intellectual bloomers." When the children were later retested, the IQ scores of the designated bloomers showed a greater gain that those of the other children. In reality, the bloomers had been selected at random: the only difference between their original scores and those of the other children was in the teachers' minds.[3]

The point to be drawn from this experiment is not (as some would maintain) that with encouragement students can raise their IQ scores, but rather that the existence of the scores assures discouragement for students from certain racial and/or socio-economic groups.

Nor is it accurate to place the onus for the discouragement on "teacher expectations." The expectations of most teachers are bound to be those of the educational system, which in turn reflect those of the society. And teachers whose expectations do not conform to the standard ones are apt to find themselves in conflict with the schools, which do indeed regard IQ tests as a "decisive piece of destiny."

A remarkable affinity exists between the view of the author who writes of the "idiotic testimony of IQ tests" and that of a college president who has asked, "Do we need more mindless testing and pseudoscientific evaluations?"[4] Clearly, many agree that we do not. In fact, not long after the president of Bard College asked this question, an education writer for *The New York Times* spoke of "a coming revolution against standardized tests."[5] Yet despite the growing reaction against IQ and other standardized tests, more and more tests are being mandated.

Increasingly over the past two decades, demands for school reform have been bound up with calls for more tests; i.e., officials assure the public that more tests are needed to guarantee scholastic "standards," "excellence," etc. But at the same time that they try to convince the public to accept more tests, they use opinion polls as evidence that the demand for more tests comes from the public.

According to a recent "Gallup Poll of the Public's Attitudes Toward the Public Schools," "Ever since 1970 people have favored national tests. . . . The sentiment for such tests seems to be a little stronger now."[6]

This conclusion was based upon the responses to the following question: "Would you like to see students in the local schools given national tests so that their educational achievement could be compared with students in other communities?"[7] The question is far from the straightforward inquiry it may appear to be. For one thing, it obliges the respondents to agree with its premise that national tests would be a measure of scholastic achievement. Thus it implicitly denies the existence of evidence demonstrating that standardized tests are a major barrier to scholastic achievement.

One wonders what changes there might have been in the yes/ no columns if the respondents had first been asked such questions as: Do you know that the drive for national tests is coming mainly from political forces, not educators? Are you aware that a prominent educator said, "Whoever controls those powerful tests will control to a large measure what is taught and learned in American schools"?[8] That another prominent educator said the multiple-choice format, which would be used in the national test, "reinforces the idea that there is a single correct answer to problems rather than encouraging people to generate alternative ideas"?[9] That standardized tests are criticized for class, racial, and sex bias?

The controversy around national tests is just one of the many offshoots of the IQ controversy, which began early in the century. Not a single one of the questions raised then has ever been resolved. As this suggests, the logical starting point for a consideration of standardized tests of any kind is a new—a different— look at IQ tests.

The IQ Mythology:
Class, Race, Gender, and Inequality

IQ:
Status of a Symbol

I

Symbolically speaking, IQ tests have been tried and found guilty time and again. Yet the tests' trials have not been only symbolic; on a number of occasions they have been real indeed. At the conclusion of one such trial—the outcome of which "sent shock waves through the testing world"[1]—the judge stated: "Defendants' expert witnesses, even those clearly affiliated with the companies that devise and distribute the standardized intelligence tests, agreed, with one exception, that we cannot truly define, much less measure, intelligence."[2]

The admission by the test companies' own witnesses that intelligence tests do not measure intelligence was, it would seem, a confession that would soon have enormous repercussions. After all, "IQ" has been used in this country as a synonym for "intelligence" longer than almost anyone can remember. To say that somebody has a "high IQ" or "low IQ" is, as everyone knows, to pass judgment on whether that person is "smart" or "dumb." If such judgments were made only about individuals as individuals, they would be damaging enough. But—because of the correspondence of IQ scores to race and class—they are not

made simply about individuals as individuals. To say that someone has a low IQ is, as a rule, to cast aspersions on that person in
a racial and/or class sense.

Obviously, there is heavy fallout from IQ tests. It moves from
the test sites, the schools—where IQ scores have been used for
generations to label children and steer them either to or away
from higher education—into the atmosphere, permeating the
country with "proof" that different races and classes are of
superior and inferior intelligence.

No Recall

Surprising as it may seem, the company witnesses' admission that
intelligence tests do not measure intelligence is not what shocked
the testing world. If, for example, the IQ-test buyers (school
officials throughout the country) had been shocked, they would
have denounced the test makers' claims as false and dangerous
and demanded a recall. Instead they continued to buy and use the
tests (except where legally constrained) just as they always had.

Actually, there was no reason to expect the testing world to be
shocked by the admission, since precedents for it had already
been set. From time to time the "mental testers," or "psychometricians," have reacted to pressure by making such admissions, which they follow up with semantic qualifications as to
what they mean by "intelligence," etc. What *did* shock both test
makers and users was the decision in the case in question.

Ruling in 1979 in *Larry P. v. Riles*, Federal District Judge Robert
F. Peckham found that IQ tests are racially and culturally biased
against blacks, and declared them unconstitutional for the use
challenged by the plaintiffs. While his decision applied to only
one test use in one state (California), its implications are universal: if IQ tests are biased against a particular group, they are not
only invalid for one use but for all uses on that group. Nor is bias
a one-dimensional phenomenon. If the tests are biased *against*
one or more groups, they are necessarily biased *in favor of* one or
more groups—and so invalid. This principle applies not only to

IQ tests but also to the tremendous range of standardized tests, all of them based on the IQ concept.

The first offshoot of the IQ test was the SAT (Scholastic Aptitude Test). Now there are so many standardized tests (variously called "ability" tests, "psychological" tests, "achievement" tests, etc.) that, it might seem, almost any accidental arrangement of nursery blocks would form the initials of one. There is, for example, the CIRCUS for children moving from preschool into first grade; the DRP to measure "reading power"; the STEP to measure "achievement" in grade school and high school; the SCAT to measure "academic ability"; the RCT to measure "competency" as a requirement for a high school diploma; the PSAT/NMSQT to qualify for a National Merit Scholarship; the SAT for college entrance. For entrance to medical school, the MCAT. For law school, the LCAT. To pass the bar, the MSBE. To get a teacher's certificate, the NTE. To get a blue-collar job, the BMCT, a test of "mechanical comprehension," which may be accompanied by the WPT, an IQ test for job applicants.

According to a recent study, 105 million standardized tests were administered to public-school students in the 1986–87 school year. This figure is conservative for a number of reasons, including that the study counted each administration of a battery of tests as only one test, even though some batteries included as many as five separate tests. Moreover, the estimated total excluded tests given in private and parochial schools, colleges, and for access to professions and jobs.[3]

More and more tests are being produced by an industry consisting of about four hundred test makers. The Educational Testing Service (ETS) is far and away the most influential component of this industry, which also includes textbook publishers, a division of IBM, and the American College Testing Program (ACT).

II

After the Peckham decision, the testers moved rapidly from shock to aggression. Pushing ahead with a campaign to extend the vast testing network, they heightened their attention to the controversy over testing, a matter that habitually preoccupies them.

One product of this heightened attention was a singular document, entitled *Ability Testing: Uses, Consequences, and Controversies* (1982). *Ability Testing*—which reveals the testing establishment's strategy—was prepared by the Committee on Ability Testing, whose members came from ETS, universities, and corporations.[4] The committee was established by the National Research Council, which is the principal operating agency of the National Academy of Sciences. It may seem surprising that the National Academy of Sciences would sponsor a report that ETS, the world's largest maker of standardized tests, was instrumental in preparing. But the academy's present relationship to testing is simply a continuation of its historical one; some seventy years ago, it played a major role in institutionalizing IQ tests.

As the Committee on Ability Testing describes it, the testing controversy is a "product of greatly expanded aspirations and contracting opportunities."[5] Thus, the mental testers suggest, those who lose out because of an inverse correlation between aspirations and opportunities are angry at the tests because the tests find them lacking in merit. This, they contend, is unfair, an attempt to slay the messenger who brings bad news. What critics must recognize, they insist, is that the test scores form a "meritocracy," and that opposition to testing is therefore without foundation.

In 1983, ETS held a conference that was followed, in 1984, by a book dealing with the major questions discussed there. One of the contributors to the volume offered a variant on the meritocracy theme, prefaced by a curious admission: "Revulsion against standardized testing has accompanied the period in which the tests have become a fixture not only in educational decision making but in entry to the labor market."

The contributor, an author and educator, ascribed the revulsion to the following "force":

One of the forces that underlies the criticism of the tests is egalitarianism, for the egalitarian complaint is that the tests discriminate among test takers and favor those with the best education and the most ability. But the force that makes standardized testing an omnipresent feature of our society is also egalitarianism, because testing continues to be the most objective mechanism available to allocate benefits.[6]

In sorting out the strands of this contradictory argument—it simultaneously treats the tests as egalitarian devices and as the means for creating a meritocracy—one finds that it converges with reality at only one point: it is true that critics charge mental tests with favoring those with the best education. But contrary to this test advocate's interpretation, it is not the critics but the psychometricians who maintain the tests favor those with the most "ability." Various test critics have, in fact, shown that the tests do not measure ability, which is one of the testers' synonyms for "intelligence."

Nor are the tests objective in any remotely scientific sense. In the special vocabulary of psychometrics, this term refers to the way standardized tests are graded, i.e., according to answers designated "right" or "wrong" when the questions are written. This definition not only overlooks that the tests contain items of opinion, which cannot be answered according to universal standards of true/false, but also overlooks that the selection of test items is an arbitrary or subjective matter.

Nor do the tests "allocate benefits." Rather, because of their class and racial biases, they sort the test takers in a way that conforms to the existing allocation, thus justifying it. This is why the tests are so vehemently defended by some and so strongly opposed by others.

"Eye" on Public Debate

Ability Testing is at once a sophisticated manual on how to defend mental testing and a document designed to exert maximum influence on the decision process. Its authors, addressing themselves to the "decision makers"—judges, legislators, educators, personnel administrators, and the testing industry[7]—state: "[W]e worked with an eye to the course of public debate and took careful notice of the state and federal legislative activities and the emerging case law."[8]

The case the Committee on Ability Testing followed with a particularly close eye was *Larry P. v. Riles*. The issue here was the use of IQ tests for assigning black children in disproportionate numbers to classes for the "educable mentally retarded" (EMR). Judge Peckham, finding that the disproportion was due to test bias, not to disproportionate mental retardation in black children, held that the tests violated the children's civil rights by leading to their segregation in special classes. IQ tests, he concluded, "doomed large numbers of black children to EMR status, racially imbalanced classes, an inferior and 'dead-end' education, and the stigma that inevitably comes from the use of the label 'retarded.'"[9]

The Committee on Ability Testing reacted to Judge Peckham's decision by warning school officials that, to preserve this testing practice—and, it may be inferred, the testing operation in general—school officials must use tests in a more sophisticated way: the "*naive* use of intelligence tests . . . to place children of linguistic or racial minority status in special education programs will not be defensible in court" (emphasis added).[10]

Even before this recommendation for a greater tactical sophistication was published, however, the testers won a victory: a judge in Illinois handed down a ruling the reverse of Judge Peckham's.[11] In attaining this decision, and in making strategic extensions in the testing network, the testers were greatly assisted by the resurgence of conservatism. As *The New York Times'* writer on education, Fred M. Hechinger, pointed out in 1983, "As usual in a conservative era, testing is in."[12]

If one were to project on the basis of testing's still-continued extension, its future would seem secure. But to project from this phenomenon would be to overlook a vital point: mental measurement is a pseudoscience, whose practice arouses "revulsion."

III

Science develops; its products keep changing and improving. Pseudoscience is static; its products remain essentially the same.

As the product of a pseudoscience that claims to measure "intelligence," "ability," "competency," etc. — which are hypothetical traits or constructs and so not subject to measurement — IQ tests have remained fundamentally the same since they were created. That current tests are basically the same as the early ones is illustrated, for example, by the criticisms made of them: contemporary charges that IQ tests are class- and race-biased and do not measure intelligence are the same ones made by the tests' earliest critics.

This country's first major critic of mental measurement was W.E.B. Du Bois. From 1910 to 1934, as editor of *The Crisis*, journal of the NAACP, Du Bois published critiques almost monthly on the testing of African-Americans.[13] Later, recalling the early days of testing, he wrote of

> the hurried use of the new technique of psychological tests, which were quickly adjusted so as to put black folk absolutely beyond the possibility of civilization. By this time I was unimpressed. I had too often seen science made the slave of caste and race hate. And it was interesting to see Odum, McDougall and Brigham eventually turn somersaults from absolute scientific proof of Negro inferiority to repudiation . . . of any test which pretended to measure innate human intelligence.[14]

In observing that intelligence tests are "adjusted" to produce desired results, Du Bois articulated a basic charge against the tests. And, in his ironic reference to the repudiation by Carl Brigham, Howard Odum, and William McDougall of their own claims that IQ tests measure "innate" intelligence, he also took note of the first of many acrobatics the testers performed as the hereditarian interpretation of IQ tests came under attack.

During the twenties, the tests were installed in the schools as instruments that allegedly measured "individual differences" in intelligence. Among the first to protest was the Chicago Federation of Labor, which in 1924 noted the "startling" correspondence between IQ-test results and the social levels of the groups tested. "The alleged 'mental levels,' representing natural ability, it will be seen, correspond in a most startling way to the social levels of the groups named. It is as though the relative social positions of each group are determined by an irresistible natural law."[15]

Acute criticisms of mental testing were also made by Walter Lippmann, who in 1922 suggested why it is a mistake to think intelligence tests measure intelligence.

> Because the results are expressed in numbers, it is easy to make the mistake of thinking that the intelligence test is a measure like a foot rule or a pair of scales . . . . Provided the foot rule and the scales agree with the . . . standard foot and standard pound in the Bureau of Standards at Washington they can be used with confidence. But intelligence is not an abstraction like length and weight; it is an exceedingly complicated notion.[16]

In pointing out that—unlike the concepts of length and weight—nothing measurable underlies the concept of intelligence, Lippmann provided the explanation for an event that would take place fifty years later: the admission by witnesses testifying for the test makers that intelligence tests do not measure intelligence.

IV

Lippmann presented his views on testing during an exchange with Lewis M. Terman, creator of the Stanford-Binet IQ test. Since Lippmann was an environmentalist and Terman a hereditarian, their encounter was an episode in the nature-nurture debate. The episode was an unusual one because it was an exchange between a journalist and a psychologist rather than between two academics, and because it appeared in a publication with a general (albeit limited) circulation, *New Republic*, of which Lippmann was then editor.

Another particularly dramatic episode in this long-running debate took place in 1969, when Arthur R. Jensen, writing in the *Harvard Educational Review*, "hypothesized" that the racial and class scoring differentials on IQ tests are mainly due to genetic differentials between races and classes.[17] The most obvious point of his article, which appeared at the end of a decade notable for its equal-rights struggles, was that children with lower IQ scores are deprived by biology of the intelligence that would entitle them to equal educational opportunities.

Jensen's revival of hereditarianism, or "scientific" racism, was sensationalized by the mass media and seized upon by powerful decision makers, who first made use of it as a rationale for cutbacks in recently launched education programs for children of lower socioeconomic status. At the same time, Jensen's thesis provoked intense opposition. In fact, so widespread was the opposition that many of the environmentalists who took issue with his genetic claims concluded that his thesis had virtually been routed. Such, as it turned out, was far from the case; the furor around his article was not followed by the retreat of biological determinism but by its continued resurgence.

The revival of hereditarianism did not, however, mark a decline in environmentalism. On the contrary, this thesis — particularly when presented in the variant known as "social pathology" — has continued to grow in influence, as can be gauged by its treatment in the mass media as well as academic journals.

Historic Warning

Not only does the debate around Jensen's thesis still have great relevance today, but so does the Lippmann-Terman encounter. Terman's presentation is significant only in that it is a prototypical hereditarian diatribe. Lippmann's contribution, however, merits special attention.

Lippmann gave a penetrating analysis of why it is impossible for IQ tests to measure intelligence, but he also stated that they may or may not measure it. Having added this touch of agnosticism, he also separated test use from test "abuse," i.e., he ventured that there might be various uses for the tests, while he criticized abuse, by which he meant the hereditarian interpretation of the results.

Yet Lippmann did not allow matters to rest there. To his great credit, he superseded the contrarieties in his position with a historic warning. If the "impression takes root that these tests really measure intelligence," declared this man who was known for his cool judgment, then "it would be a thousand times better if all the intelligence testers and all their questionnaires were sunk without warning in the Sargasso Sea."[18]

The environmentalists who came after Lippmann have, on the one hand, done valuable work in exposing the hereditarians' activities and, to an extent, their ideas. On the other hand, with few exceptions, they have not heeded Lippmann's grave warning.[19] Instead of abandoning IQ tests if the impression he feared took root, they have accepted them as a measure of intelligence. At the same time that they have ignored his warning, they have expanded on his contrarieties; for example, they generally attribute the many ills with which testing is identified to test abuse, or misuse, and offer a variety of suggestions that would supposedly lead to improvement.

Originally, the testing establishment regarded the abuse/misuse question as anathema. But finally the testers realized that if one ascribes the problems mental tests are blamed for to test misuse, one does not reject but rather accept psychometrics. Thus they themselves now profess concern with test misuse: the ETS conference in 1983 was called "The Uses and Misuses of Tests."

But there are also others—test critics whose objectives clearly conflict with those of the testers—who speak in terms of test misuse. Yet the problems these critics are deeply concerned with—as this new look at mental tests will show—cannot be ameliorated within the framework of psychometrics, but only intensified by this inherently biased pseudoscience. In fact, it seems a misnomer for such critics to speak of test misuse, since they themselves have made fundamental criticisms of testing and have also supported, or even initiated, various legal actions against standardized tests.

V

Although the start of the hereditarian-environmentalist debate long preceded IQ testing, it has for most of the twentieth century revolved around the tests, i.e., over whether the racial and class scoring differentials, assumed to be intelligence differentials, should be attributed mainly to heredity or mainly to environment. In a review of yet another addition to the voluminous literature on this subject, the reviewer observed "how frozen the argument has become."[20] If anything, this observation understates the case. The debate has not simply *become* frozen but has—for reasons we shall explore—remained at the point where it began.

Interdependent Myths

Like IQ tests, the hereditarian-environmentalist debate is immersed in mythology. In fact, the debate has revolved around IQ testing for so long that the myths surrounding each are not only intertwined but interdependent.

According to its image, the nature-nurture debate pits conservatives against liberals. One part of this image reflects reality; hereditarians as a group are certainly conservative. But another part is mythical; environmentalism has not only liberal and radical supporters, but many conservative ones as well.

One factor that sustains the debate's liberal-versus-conservative image is that many environmentalists have condemned the hereditarians' claims of genetic intelligence differentials between races and classes as a justification for class and racial inequality. At the same time, however, environmentalists present their own thesis—which accepts the claim of class and racial intelligence differentials, but attributes the alleged differentials to environment rather than heredity—as an alternative to hereditarianism. But is their thesis in fact an alternative to hereditarianism? Or does it instead—irrespective of the intentions of many environmentalists—result in an alternative justification for class and racial inequality?

These questions lie below the surface of the IQ controversy.

IQ's Skeletons

I

IQ testing has a skeleton in the closet. Lots of them: the forebear of twentieth-century psychometrics was nineteenth-century craniometrics. As Stephen Jay Gould pointed out in 1974, "The racist arguments of the nineteenth century were primarily based on craniometry, the measurement of human skulls. Today, these contentions stand totally discredited. What craniometry was to the nineteenth century, intelligence testing has been to the twentieth."[1]

By making this analogy between craniometry and intelligence testing, Gould—the biologist, geologist, and Harvard professor—both indicted IQ testing and provided historical evidence that this pseudoscience too is fated to stand totally discredited.

Seven years after making the analogy, Gould published *The Mismeasure of Man*. Contrary to what one might expect, the book did not take up where the analogy left off. Gould no longer defined intelligence testing as the modern counterpart of craniometry. Instead, he disassociated psychometrics from its long-discredited forebear and proceeded to a defense of IQ testing. This may seem surprising, given that *The Mismeasure of Man* is often taken as a challenge to mental measurement. But the clue to the book's position is in its title: by saying that "man" has been *mis*measured, it suggests that man can also be *properly* measured.

13

In *The Mismeasure of Man*, Gould substituted a profoundly qualified analogy between craniometrics and psychometrics for his original one. Before considering the replacement, let us look at craniometrics itself.

Looking Back

There is often a tendency to look back with derision at the pseudosciences of the past. How naive people must have been to believe in anything so ridiculous! Yet what appears as naiveté may be at least as much a product of social conditioning as of lack of knowledge. Craniometry, which seems so ludicrous today, was not introduced by marginal but mainstream figures, whose assets were scientific credentials from other areas.

Craniometry was accepted as a science and praised by the standard setters of the time. Moreover, its acceptance as a science persisted long after critics exposed it from both scientific and social standpoints. That craniometry could go on in the face of such exposure can be explained in only one way: its ability to provide a "scientific" justification for the arrangements of the social order.[2]

The craniometricians, who began functioning in this country during slavery, contended that differentials in social status between races, classes, and the sexes were the result of differentials in brain size. To "prove" that upper-class whites and black slaves were biologically suited to their places at polar ends of the social hierarchy, the craniometricians did not hesitate to manipulate their measurements.

But manipulation was unnecessary to demonstrate that men's brains are larger than women's, since in fact they tend to be. But the real evidence of a sex differential in brain size was as worthless as the faked evidence of racial and class differentials: if brain size correlated with intelligence, some animals would be smarter than human beings. What brain size actually tends to correlate with is body size.

Craniometrics was practiced in two main forms: phrenology,

which came on the scene first, and craniology. Although both the craniologists and phrenologists were concerned with total skull size, the latter's special interest was measuring different parts of the skull. The phrenologists believed that each mental trait or "faculty" is controlled by a specific "organ" of the brain, and that a protuberance at a designated place on the skull denoted an ample endowment of that trait and an indentation the opposite.

The phrenologists, as the first practitioners of craniometrics, "laid the groundwork" for the psychometricians, observed Stephan L. Chorover, MIT professor of psychology and brain science: "It was the phrenologists—long before Binet invented the intelligence scale—who first maintained that traits like intelligence were amenable to quantitative measurement. Thus phrenology laid the groundwork for all subsequent efforts to assign numerical values to human behavior."[3]

A Reanalysis

In *The Mismeasure of Man,* Gould told of his reanalysis of the craniologists' activities (he did not deal with the phrenologists). His revealing review of their work showed the lengths to which they went in trying to make their results match their prior assumptions about a biological ranking of races. Gould points out that Samuel Morton (1799–1851), an American professor of anatomy and a paleontologist as well as a craniologist, used an accommodating measure, mustard seed, which could easily have been filtered loosely through blacks' skulls and tamped down tightly in Caucasian ones. Gould also tells how the craniologist Paul Broca (1824–1880)—who was also a neurologist, a professor of clinical surgery, and the founder of the Anthropological Society of Paris in 1859—switched from one physical criterion to another in a losing effort to support his prior claims that these criteria offered proof of white, upper-class, and male superiority.

The "scientific" culture out of which craniometry emerged

was marked by the concepts of the early biological determinists. In *The Mismeasure of Man*, Gould copiously documented and analyzed their notions and their doings, as well as those of early twentieth-century biological determinists. "Yet [his] analysis is somehow incomplete," observed R.C. Lewontin, the evolutionary geneticist and Harvard professor of zoology and biology.

> With its emphasis on the racism of individual scientists . . . , *The Mismeasure of Man* remains a curiously unpolitical and unphilosophical book. Morton, Broca, [Cesare] Lombroso, [Henry] Goddard [and others] make their appearance as if from a closet, and smelling a bit of mothballs. They are "men of their time," displaying antique social prejudices which on occasion come back to haunt us in the form of "criminal chromosomes" and a brief eruption of Jensenism. Their biological determinism appears as a disarticulated cultural artifact, nasty and curious . . . but not integrated into any structure of social relations.[4]

If certain figures from the past displayed no more than antiquated social prejudices, we might relax and smile over the distance we have traveled from past to present. Lewontin warned us not to. The prejudices that may seem so reassuringly antique in *The Mismeasure of Man* are alive today, if not well, because they have been transmitted from past to present by the practices and processes known as institutional racism. And the practice of IQ testing—as Gould's 1974 analogy made so evident—has the same bearing on these processes as craniometry did in earlier times.

Continuing with his critique of *The Mismeasure of Man*, Lewontin stated: "In America, race, ethnicity and class are so confounded, and the reality of social class so firmly denied, that it is easy to lose sight of the general setting of class conflict out of which biological determinism arose."[5]

In this country, biological determinism arose when the slave-owning class was on the rise. But instead of diminishing with the end of slavery, the influence of this thesis grew stronger. At the beginning of the twentieth century, it helped create a receptive atmosphere for the introduction of the new, more sophisticated pseudoscience that replaced craniometrics.

II

While Gould's analogy of 1974 told us that intelligence testing has the same relationship to the racist arguments of the twentieth century as craniometry had to those of the nineteenth, the analogy he offered in *The Mismeasure of Man* made a different point: "What craniometry was for the nineteenth century, intelligence testing has become for the twentieth, when it assumes that intelligence (or at least a dominant part of it) is a single, innate, heritable, and measurable thing."[6]

Instead of repudiating intelligence testing, as he did in his original analogy, Gould now accepted it so long as the testers did not assume that intelligence is a "single, innate, heritable, and measurable thing." In taking issue with the claim that intelligence is measurable as a single, etc., *thing*—but *not* with the claim that intelligence is measurable—Gould argued against the hereditarian approach of *reifying* intelligence, or treating this abstraction as something real.

By criticizing the measurement of intelligence as a single trait, Gould suggested that it is valid to quantify it as a number of traits (a point he went on to develop). By this standard, phrenology would have been valid because it measured mental worth as a number of quantities. By the same standard, craniology would have been invalid because it measured mental worth as a single quantity, and not because it made the pseudoscientific assumption that mental worth can be quantified.

By qualifying his 1974 analogy, Gould obscured the connection he originally revealed when he stated that "What craniometry was to the nineteenth century, intelligence testing has been to the twentieth." And, having severed mental measurement per se from its repudiated predecessor, Gould proceeded to his defense of IQ testing, which he centered upon Alfred Binet.

Founding Father

The French psychologist Alfred Binet (1857–1911) personified the link between craniometrics and psychometrics. Inspired by Broca, Binet spent years trying to validate head size as a measure of intelligence by establishing a correlation between it and school performance, which craniologists also assumed to be a measure of intelligence. In 1900, when craniology was making its exit, he acknowledged the failure of his efforts. In 1904, he received a commission from France's minister of public instruction to devise a means for deciding which pupils should be sent to what would now be called classes for the educable mentally retarded. He fulfilled his commission by creating an "intelligence scale."

Although controversy has swirled around intelligence tests for generations, Binet—who created the prototype—has virtually been absolved of responsibility for their consequences. And not only has he been absolved. In the writings of environmentalists as well as hereditarians, Binet emerges as a protagonist. While hereditarians generally praise the test he created, contemporary environmentalists usually praise one or another of his ideas. Gould did both.

"Binet's Principles"

With his 1974 analogy, Gould placed intelligence testing in the category of pseudoscience. In *The Mismeasure of Man*, he reclassified it as a science, and ascribed what he called the "momentous consequences"[7] of testing to a violation of "Binet's principles": "If Binet's principles had been followed, and his tests consistently used as he intended, we would have been spared a major misuse of science in our century."[8]

Gould attributed a number of principles to Binet. For example, he asserted that Binet was an antihereditarian;[9] that he tested to "help and improve, not to label";[10] that he intended his test to be used only for the "limited purpose of his commission," and "refused to regard" it as a "general device for ranking all pupils according to mental worth."[11]

Even on its own terms, Gould's argument is contradictory. For instance, he tried to back up his claim that Binet intended his test to be used only for the purpose of his commission by quoting Binet, who said that the "most valuable use of our scale" would be its application to pupils of "inferior grades of intelligence."[12] The quotation, however, undermines Gould's denial that Binet labeled children.

To support his classification of Binet as an antihereditarian, Gould cited a statement that figures prominently in writings by environmentalists. In this remark, Binet—rejecting the hereditarian view that his test measures intelligence as a *fixed* quantity—asserted; "We must protest and react against this brutal pessimism."[13] Although this seems a humane declaration, Binet was actually insisting that protest be confined to the hereditarian interpretation of the test, thus exempting mental testing itself from the charge of brutality. At the same time, Binet set the stage for a debate that continues in full force today—a debate in which both sides accept the tests' verdict that certain populations are inferior in intelligence and argue over whether their intelligence is fixed or can be "boosted."

But Binet by no means confined himself to expressing environmentalist views. He claimed, for example, that his test was designed to "separate natural intelligence and instruction" because it is "the intelligence alone that we seek to measure."[14] Gould tried to explain away this classical hereditarian claim by saying that Binet's "obvious desire" was to "remove the superficial effects of clearly acquired knowledge" from test scores.[15] It should, however, be clear that *all* knowledge is acquired, and the presence or lack of it affects test scores. Gould's disclaimer mystified rather than described what Binet tried to do—that is, formulate his test so it was not apparent that it called for certain skills and information, and thus could be claimed to measure "intelligence alone."

In portraying Binet as an antihereditarian, Gould also stated that Binet abandoned craniology because he failed to find a correlation between head size and school performance.[16] Had Binet abandoned craniology for this reason, it would have been a purely pragmatic step, not one that implied abandonment of its hereditarian precepts. But in fact Binet did not abandon craniology. In 1910, after having published two versions of his test, he recommended the use of cephalometry, or head measurement, to "confirm" the test's results: "When a child, according to tests made in class or in a regular psychological examination, appears to have little intelligence, this judgment, always delicate and complicated, can be weighed and confirmed by cephalometry."[17]

Original Use

By asserting that Binet's test should have been used only as he intended and that Binet intended it to be used only for the "limited purpose of his commission," Gould was of course recommending that IQ tests be used in this way today. The recommendation is of special significance because the use in question is the one Judge Peckham ruled against.

Binet was commissioned, as Gould described it, to "develop techniques for identifying those children whose lack of success in normal classrooms suggested the need for some form of special education."[18] It is difficult, if not impossible, to understand from this ambiguous description what the techniques were supposed to do. Identifying children who lacked success in school? Obviously not; they were already identified by their school performance. Identifying children who needed special education? Apparently not; unsuccessful school performance, it seems, suggests a need for special education. But one thing is clear: those who commissioned Binet assumed that something is wrong with the children whose school performance is unsuccessful.

But why assume that unsuccessful school performance means something is wrong with the children? Why should unsuccessful school performance, particularly when it is widespread, not suggest that something is wrong with the schools? Clearly, the officials who commissioned Binet would never have entertained such a suggestion. They already "knew" the reason for lack of scholastic success: lack of intelligence.

They also knew that Binet was committed to this belief, as attested by his background in comparing head size with school performance. It is thus perfectly logical that they gave their commission to Binet, who fulfilled it by producing an intelligence scale that "scientifically" shifted the onus for school performance from school officials to school children. The significance of this shift becomes particularly apparent when an intelligence test is used as Binet originally intended, i.e., for classifying children as mentally retarded and moving them from regular classes to special ones.

Gould also presented Binet's ideas for special education. Binet, as Gould described it, believed special education "must be tailored to the individual needs of disadvantaged children."[19] Although clearly intended to show that Binet felt compassion for poor children, this remark instead revealed his class bias; he made the prior assumption that the children in the special classes would not come from the school population as a whole, but only from its lower socioeconomic sectors. He then devised a test that supported the assumption.

For the special classes, Binet proposed an authoritarian regimen: "lessons of will, of attention, of discipline."[20] According to Gould, Binet viewed such lessons as "prerequisites" for academic pursuits.[21] In reality, the special program Binet envisioned could only cause children to fall further behind scholastically—i.e., it was not designed to deal with school subjects but with the children's presupposed deficits.

Binet also called for fifteen to twenty pupils in the special classes rather than the sixty to eighty then typical of classes in schools for poor children. This proposal sounds quite impressive, but it raises the question of why Binet did not recommend a reduction in the size of the regular classes for poor children. Had he done so, he would have acknowledged what his test denied, that is, the connection between school conditions and school performance. So far as the children in special classes go, the issue is no longer class size, but that, in Judge Peckham's words, they have been "doomed" to "'dead-end' education," and given the "stigma that inevitably comes from the use of the label 'retarded.'"

In his writings, Binet did not limit his recommendations to special education, but also made some with obviously general implications. For instance, he proposed the following: "Certain children, to whom the ordinary work of the class is distasteful, make compensation in manual work . . . little girls weak in orthography, are strong in sewing and capable in the instruction concerning housekeeping; and, all things considered, this is more important for their future."[22]

Thus Binet, displaying the kind of logic the testers have since become noted for, overlooked the connection between the overcrowding of schools and the pupils' distaste for school, and inferred that the distaste is caused by a lack of scholastic aptitude.

Binet's claim that certain children have an aptitude for housework or manual labor rather than for academic pursuits is so bald, so dated, as to make sexism and class bias seem like antique prejudices. This is rather ironic, given that the descendents of the test he created are a significant means for transmitting those biases today.

Ideal City

There is yet another facet to Gould's argument that the momentous consequences of IQ testing could have been avoided if Binet's principles had been followed, namely, his claim that Binet "refused to regard" his test as a "general device for ranking all pupils according to mental worth."

First, it was inevitable that Binet's test, irrespective of Binet's own attitude, would be used as a device for general ranking—or, to put it another way, that the test's original use would set a precedent in a microcosm for the test's universal use.

Although Binet's original aim was to construct an instrument for classifying unsuccessful school performers inferior in intelligence, it was impossible for him to create one that would do only that, i.e., function at only one extreme. Because his test was a projection of the relationship between the concepts of inferiority and superiority—each of which requires the other—it was intrinsically a device for universal ranking according to alleged mental worth.

Since all IQ-test scores are relative, or inherently dependent on each other, it is illogical to contend, as Gould did, that one test use is beneficial and the others are not. To be logical one must acknowledge that if the original test use was positive, as Gould maintained, then the others would be too. Conversely, if other test uses are negative, as Gould suggested in this instance (although not in others), then something was wrong with the original use, that is, intrinsically wrong with the test.

Although Binet's opposition could not have prevented the general use of his test, the fact is that he did not oppose but advocated it. When Binet said that the "most valuable use of our scale" would be its application on "pupils of inferior grades of intelligence," he implied that it would also have other valuable uses on pupils. Yet he did not leave matters at that, but instead went on to visualize universal applications:

> Of what use is a measure of intelligence? Without doubt one could conceive many possible applications of the process in dreaming of a future where the social sphere would be better organized than ours; where everyone would work according to his known aptitudes in such a way that no particle of psychic force should be lost for society. That would be the ideal city.[23]

There is something strange about Binet's dream. He spoke rhapsodically of an ideal city, but he was silent about the extreme inequities in existing ones. And his sole stipulation for his ideal society—that everyone be tested and work according to his or her "known aptitudes"—would not alleviate but perpetuate the inequities.

When Binet asserted that everyone would work according to "known" aptitudes, he was saying that the individuals comprising a particular group would work according to the aptitudes that group was "known" to have. When he suggested, for example, that children of lower socioeconomic status are perfectly suited to manual labor, he was simply expressing what elite groups "know," that is, that they themselves have mental aptitudes, and other groups have manual ones. It was this elitist belief, this universal rationale for the social status quo, that would be upheld by the universal testing Binet proposed.

At the same time that Binet portrayed the meritocratic ideal, he also revealed, albeit inadvertently, the grim reality it conceals. In the year that he published the first version of his intelligence scale, he stated that when his work "became definitive," it would "permit the solution of many current questions, since it is no less a matter than the measurement of intelligence . . . permitting comparisons not only according to age, but also according to sex, social conditions, race, intellectual status . . . and normal and criminal anthropology."[24]

Binet's prediction was soon fulfilled by the psychometricians. Claiming to seek solutions to social problems, they produced measurements to support the long-standing assumption that mental worth is relative to class, race, and sex.

IQ Takes Over

I

The speed with which mental tests moved from their creation in France to their use on a mass scale in the United States is quite remarkable, particularly in view of the strikingly slower tempo of those times. Consider the following chronology.

1909. The 1908 version of the Binet test was translated, published, and administered by Henry Goddard. Goddard, the prototype of the early testers in this country, was a social Darwinist. He initially administered the test to 400 youthful inmates of a home for the "feebleminded" in Vineland, New Jersey.

1910–1911. The first of the racial comparisons called for by Binet took place. In Vineland, Goddard tested two thousand white children in the public schools. In Philadelphia, the board of education commissioned Howard Odum to test black children, then entering the city's schools in increasing numbers, and compare the results with Goddard's tests of white children.

1912. Against a background of mounting efforts to halt the "new immigrants"—a massive wave of southern and eastern Europeans—the U.S. Public Health Service commissioned Goddard to administer the test to arrivals at Ellis Island. After the testing, Goddard announced that 87 percent of the Russians, 83 percent of the Jews, 80 percent of the Hungarians, and 79 percent of the Italians were feebleminded. Soon deportations began to spiral wildly, with Goddard reporting a 350 percent increase in 1913 and 570 percent in 1914.

1916. Terman published the Stanford-Binet. An adaptation of Binet's final version of his intelligence scale (1911), it was to become known as the first IQ test. According to Terman, the test had "found" that "children of superior social status yield a higher average mental age than children of the laboring classes."[1] In addition to announcing his claims about class intelligence differentials, Terman also declared that the tests had shown a "borderline" deficiency in intelligence to be "very, very common among Spanish-Indian and Mexican families of the Southwest, and among negroes." Predicting that "enormously significant racial differences in general intelligence" would be "discovered" by future tests, he advised that children of "this group should be segregated in special classes," where they "can often be made efficient workers." He went on to lament that there "is no possibility at present of convincing society that they should not be allowed to reproduce, although from a eugenic point of view, they constitute a grave problem."[2] Interestingly, at the time he made these remarks, three states (including his own) had already passed eugenic sterilization laws. He himself was a leader of the eugenics movement.

1917. As the United States entered World War I, Robert Yerkes, a Harvard psychology professor, president of the American Psychological Association, and a leader of the eugenics movement, won approval from the military of a program to test draftees. Together with Terman, Goddard, and other hereditarians, Yerkes constructed two IQ-type tests: the Alpha for literates and the Beta for nonliterates (the latter category included those who could not read English). These tests, which were based on such standard educational materials of the time as *McGuffey's Readers* and *Poor Richard's Almanac*, were given to 1.75 million soldiers.

1920. Yerkes and C.S. Yoakum published *Army Mental Tests*, an analysis authorized by the War Department. Declaring that the army tests were "definitely known" to "measure native intellectual ability," the authors reported that the draftees had been classified into grades A through E, representing mental ages ranging from nineteen years down to ten years.[3] Those in category C were deemed "rarely capable of finishing a high school course."[4] Twenty-five percent of the draftees were placed in this category and about 45 percent in lower ones.

1921. The National Academy of Sciences published an 875-page statistical analysis of the scores of more than 160 thousand draftees.[5] According to this report, which Yerkes edited, the "average" white draftee had a mental age of 13 years, or was just above the edge of "moronity." Eighty-nine percent of the African-American, most of the southern and eastern European, and 37 percent of the white draftees were categorized as morons. The report also associated intelligence with class by including a table in which army assignments ranging from "engineer officer" down to "laborer" were correlated with descending mental ages. Congress, as a temporary measure, placed its first limitation on immigration. The test statistics also "armed the opponents of social advances with new arguments against bettering the status quo in government health, education, and family welfare systems."[6]

1923. Carl Brigham, a Princeton psychologist, published *A Study of American Intelligence*, in which he warned of a "decline of American intelligence." Declaring that the army test results indicate a "definite" superiority of the Nordic group, he urged restrictions on countries with other-than-Nordic populations. But, he insisted, unless these steps were accompanied by eugenic measures, "The decline of American intelligence will be more rapid than the decline of the intelligence of European national groups, owing to the presence here of the negro."[7] In a foreword, Yerkes warned that no citizen "can afford to ignore the menace of race deterioration."[8] The number of eugenic sterilization laws was climbing (by the early 1940s, thirty states would have them). Testimony inspired by the WWI tests and Brigham's book was presented to the House Committee on Immigration and Naturalization.

1924. More of the same kind of testimony was presented to the House committee.[9] Later that year, Congress passed the Immigration Act, restricting the entry of all but Nordic immigrants.[10] Now the mental testing movement was riding high. Chorover writes: "The open door, which had offered the chance of a new life to millions of immigrants, was closing as Congress [fashioned] a new immigration law, and the mental testing movement finally came into its own."[11]

II

How does the Committee on Ability Testing of the National Academy of Sciences look back on the Academy's 1921 report? Not, by any means, in anger.

To be sure, the authors expressed a certain disapproval of the sins of the past, i.e., of the "xenophobic sentiments" of the post-WWI period.[12] At the same time, however, they attempted to distance the earlier report from these sentiments by contending that its "findings" were "picked up by anti-immigrationists."[13] Thus they implied that the report itself — which ranked races and nationalities into an alleged hierarchy of intelligence — was an objective document that was misused.

According to the committee, the army tests were an "experiment," which seems an odd description of a project involving almost two million men. In any event, if these tests were an experiment, the reason was not that the testers sought to discover anything. Their objective was to demonstrate that group tests, which were necessary if testing was to become general, could produce results corresponding to those from individually administered tests, whose reliability in yielding the desired outcomes had already been established. Because the group tests given to the WWI draftees showed this could be done, they are regarded as a landmark by the testing establishment.

The Committee on Ability Testing also recommended that readers turn for a description of the "racial theories that were part of the intellectual atmosphere in which testing was developed" to *The Mismeasure of Man*.[14]

III

In *The Mismeasure of Man*, Gould discussed the racial theories, or individual variations on a hereditarian theme, of Terman, Brigham, Yerkes, et al.

In his treatment of Yerkes, for instance, Gould presented samples of that tester's biological-determinist views, but devoted his attention mainly to "Yerkes's report of the summary statistics," i.e., the Academy's report on the army tests. As Gould described it, these data had a "rotten core."[15] Why? Because the tests were administered under "Draconian conditions" and because the testers engaged in manipulation that, for example, allowed them to come up with thirteen as the average mental age for white draftees—a statistical absurdity. The "fallacies and finagling that thoroughly invalidated" this figure "remained hidden" in the details of the massive report.[16] From this statement, one may well conclude that Gould rejected the army-test statistics. But such is not the case.

In holding that the statistics were invalid because they were the product of finagling and fallacies, Gould restricted his criticism to the early testers' deviations from "normal" procedures or, to put it conversely, he suggested that intelligence can be quantified so long as approved procedures are followed. Because he accepted the fallacious premise of mental measurement, he could overlook his technical criticism and, paradoxically, accept the figures he had apparently rejected; although the product of deviant methods, they nonetheless ranked races and classes in the same way as those produced by approved methods.

That Gould *did* accept the figures he had called "rotten" is evident from the fact that he also described them as "pure numbers." "As pure numbers, these data carried no inherent social message. They might have been used to promote equality of opportunity."[17]

Gould did not explain why he called the same figures both "rotten" and "pure." He did, however, maintain that they could, in his opinion, have been used to promote "equality of opportunity" if Yerkes had argued that "an average mental age of thirteen reflected the fact that relatively few recruits had the opportunity to finish or even to attend high school."[18] In other words, Yerkes should have turned his argument around; instead of taking the hereditarian view that the draftees had not acquired a higher level of education because they had a low level of intelligence, he should have taken the environmentalist view that a group's level of intelligence is largely determined by its level of education. Of course, when a group is deemed deficient in intelligence, whether for environmental or genetic reasons, its members are considered unprepared for equal education and consigned to an inferior one.

In the many decades since the first army tests, a great number of tests have been interpreted from an environmentalist standpoint, yet there is no instance when the tests have helped to promote equality of opportunity. Nor could there ever be. It is paradoxical to maintain that IQ tests, which are inherently biased, can promote equal opportunity. The tests do what their construction dictates; they correlate a group's mental worth with its place in the social hierarchy.

The WWI statistics are a case in point. Far from being pure or value-free numbers that acquired meaning only when interpreted along hereditarian lines, they were the product of certain values—the values of men who visualized an intelligence scale on which Nordics were ranked above Slavs and African-Americans below everyone else, and who directed their efforts toward upholding their preconceptions.

Dream Come True

At the same time that Gould maintained the WWI statistics could have been put to good use, he also reiterated his contention that mass testing contradicted Binet's aim: with the construction of the army tests, "Binet's purpose" could be "circumvented" because a "technology had been developed" for universal testing.[19]

In reality, the army tests allowed Binet's vision of mass testing not only to be realized, but to be realized in exactly the way that would have pleased him most. Binet was eager for his test to be adapted for use by the military—so eager that he asked France's minister of war to institute trial testing in the army. "Binet has told us enough to know that some of these tests were carried out, yet it was in the United States Army in 1917 that these dreams of his saw their fruition," related his biographer, Theta H. Wolf.[20]

Although the U.S. Army tested almost two million men, Gould did not believe it "ever made much use" of the tests for assigning personnel, except in some specific situations.[21] The Committee on Ability Testing makes the same point, stating that the tests had "little effect" on the "placement of personnel."[22] But the fact that the tests had little effect on assignments should not be construed to mean the army made little use of them.

On the contrary, the tests' very lack of effect on the placement of personnel provides the clue to their use. The tests were used to justify, not alter, the army's traditional personnel policy, which called for the selection of officers from among relatively affluent whites and the assignment of whites of lower socioeconomic status to lower-status roles and African-Americans to the bottom rung.

IV

The mental testers' eagerness to call attention to the scoring differentials on the WWI tests between blacks and whites, native- and foreign-born, as well as officers and enlisted men, was matched by their anxiety to hide or explain away certain by-products of their statistics. One such by-product was the scoring differential between southern blacks and northern blacks.

To justify this gap, which in itself was an affront to the genetic

interpretation, the hereditarians devised the "selective migration" thesis, according to which blacks who migrated to the
North were biologically superior to those who stayed in the
South. If this explanation simply ignored that the North-South
scoring differential also applied to whites, well, hereditarians
have never been overly concerned with their gaps in logic.

One of the first to refute the selective-migration thesis was the
educator Horace Mann Bond. Writing in *The Crisis* in 1924, Bond
pointed out that the explanation for the northern black–southern
black scoring differential lay "above all" in the differentials in
"school conditions."[23] These differentials were traceable to the
fact that—although there was de facto school segregation in the
North, and northern states, too, spent more on educating whites
than blacks—northern states spent more than southern ones on
educating both blacks and whites.

In 1935, another significant step was taken in answering the
hereditarians' claim that the army tests measured "innate"
intelligence: the psychologist Otto Klineberg published a comparison of the median Alpha scores for blacks from four northern states and whites from four southern ones. It showed that
the blacks from the northern states had outscored the whites
from the southern ones.[24] Klineberg also cited figures showing
the differentials in the southern states' expenditures for educating African-Americans and whites, as well as the greater amount
the North spent on education.

The next significant step in the refutation process occurred in
1945, when Ashley Montagu published a new analysis of the
army scores.[25] Having found that no further median scores for
blacks and whites had been computed after Klineberg's four-
state comparison, he set out to calculate the missing majority.
Although he discovered that no statistics existed for black
draftees in twenty-five states, he was able to calculate black and
white Alpha median scores for nineteen more states and the
District of Columbia; he also calculated medians for the Beta.
With the additional median scores, trends that were indicated by
the earlier comparisons—and that hereditarians claimed were

based on too little data to be representative—emerged as well-defined patterns.

The added medians for the Alpha showed that blacks from four northern states did better than whites from nine southern ones. The score ranks for the Beta generally correlated quite highly with those from the Alpha. Montagu also computed comprehensive median scores for draftees who took the Alpha plus the Beta or an individual examination, or all three. These scores, too, showed that northern blacks did better than whites from many southern states; Ohio blacks, for example, outscored whites from *eleven* southern states. Montagu's analysis also brought other striking facts to light; it showed, for example, that Ohio blacks did better on the Alpha than whites from nine *northern* states. Had testing data been available for blacks from every state, it is clear that there would have been even more evidence to confound the mental testers' preconceptions.

The distribution of scores over the states showed that the lowest ones for both African-Americans and whites were achieved by draftees from the deep South. "[T]he deeper the South the lower the score," Montagu observed. Commenting on the cause of this phenomenon, he stated,

> The depressed socio-economic state of the South as compared with the greater part of the rest of the United States is an unfortunate fact. It is, therefore, not surprising that both Negroes and whites in the South should do worse on the tests than their fellows in any other part of the Union; and, since conditions are invariably worse for Negroes than for whites, that the Negroes should do worse than the whites.[26]

In reading Montagu's study almost half a century after its publication, one is struck by its systematic refutation of basic hereditarian claims, and also by another feature: Montagu did not replace the rejected hereditarian arguments with environmentalist ones, but diverged from them in significant ways. For example, while the environmentalist position accepts the claim that IQ tests measure intelligence, Montagu regarded the claim as dubious, i.e., he spoke of "intelligence, or whatever it was that was measured by these tests."[27] While the environmentalist view takes IQ scores as evidence that racial differentials in socioeconomic conditions produce racial differentials in *intelligence*, Montagu pointed to the effect of unequal socioeconomic conditions on *scores*—i.e., on the outcome of tests whose validity as a measure of intelligence he simultaneously placed under suspicion.

V

By the end of the 1920s, when the environmentalist position had begun to assume greater importance, at least some of the mental testers started to make an important adjustment. They realized there was little reason to fear environmentalism, given its acceptance of IQ tests as a measure of intelligence. As a result, psychometrics began its move away from an exclusive identification with hereditarianism to one with environmentalism as well. One of the first of the hereditarians to signal the coming realignment was Brigham.

When Du Bois said that Brigham turned "somersaults," he was referring to Brigham's retraction, in 1930, of his analysis of the army tests. Gould also dealt with Brigham's retraction, but interpreted it in an entirely different way. In Gould's opinion, the recantation was prompted by a "profound change of heart";[28] for "each error, [Brigham] apologized with an abjectness rarely encountered in scientific literature";[29] thus he "paid his personal debt."[30]

Since the recantation is relevant today, it is worth determining whether its author had a profound change of heart or merely turned somersaults. First, the recantation was preceded by a great deal of criticism. (This included criticism of the hereditarians' claims about foreign-born draftees, whose scores were found to correlate with the length of time they had spent in this country and its schools.) And the criticism, to which Brigham

reacted selectively, did not come only from opponents of hereditarianism. In 1928, Truman Kelley, a hereditarian, published a
critique of the army tests on methodological grounds. "It was
Kelley's critique that apparently proved overwhelming to Brigham, whose 1930 repudiation leaned heavily on it for documentation," observed Douglas Lee Eckberg, a sociologist.[31]

If Brigham had had a profound change of heart, and attempted to pay his personal debt, he would have called for
repeal of the immigration-restriction and eugenic-sterilization
laws he had crusaded for. But he did not. Nor did he offer an
apology for his rantings about "race deterioration." In fact, he
made no mention of blacks, even though he had reserved his
ultimate slander for them. His qualified retraction—an article
titled "Intelligence Tests of Immigrant Groups"—was written in
a technical manner and appeared in *The Psychological Review*,[32] a
journal unknown to a public that had been exposed by the mass
media to Brigham's original claims.

In the article, Brigham criticized not only the construction of
the Alpha and Beta, but also the fact that he had combined their
results into a single scale on the assumption they were equivalent tests. Because of his use of this method, he declared, his
"study with its entire hypothetical superstructure of racial differences collapses completely."[33] At first glance this appears to
be a sweeping repudiation, but upon closer examination a
question arises: Was Brigham saying his hypothesis of racial
intelligence differentials had collapsed, or merely that the hypothetical superstructure of this particular study had collapsed?

His explicit answer was that his original study was "without
foundation" because "[c]omparative studies of various national
and racial groups may not be made with existing tests."[34] So
instead of repudiating mental tests as a means for making
invidious comparisons between races and nationalities, Brigham suggested that new tests be constructed to make them.

Further, pending construction of such tests, he proposed an
adjusted approach to existing ones. Since psychologists "have
been attacked because of their use of the term 'intelligence,'"

they should no longer speak of an intelligence-test score as a measure of intelligence. Instead, "Their definition of intelligence must now be [a] 'score in a test which we *consider* to measure intelligence'" (emphasis added).[35] The suggestion was a seminal one for the mental testers, who would come to rely more and more on semantics to parry criticism.

Nor did Brigham's subsequent work reflect a change of heart. At the time of his retraction, he had already become secretary of the College Entrance Examination Board. In this capacity, he devised the SAT, which, as an alleged measure of scholastic aptitude, has served as an adjunct to IQ tests for making class, racial, and gender comparisons of mental worth.

Brigham rendered special services to the testing establishment, and it has honored him accordingly. The ETS library bears his name.

The IQ Hierarchy

I

With their first mass testing project behind them, the psychometricians were ready for their next giant step, namely, full-scale testing in the schools. Offering the testers' classic interpretation of this move, the Committee on Ability Testing stated, "Schools could use intelligence tests to . . . arrange students in a hierarchy of ability groupings."[1]

If, as the committee maintained, IQ tests arrange students in a hierarchy of ability groupings, testing has created a meritocracy in the schools. But in making this assertion, the committee omitted the salient point that the presumably new arrangements of the testing era corresponded in essence to the preexisting ones, which segregated students by race and divided them by class.

IQ tests were in fact introduced at a time when the schools were coming under increasing fire for segregation and for sorting students along class lines. With the advent of testing, a change occurred. The school authorities could now "prove" what they had always claimed: that the hierarchy in the schools, like that of the social order itself, was based on individual merit, whose presence or absence, perhaps unfortunately but nonetheless inescapably, happened to correspond to the individual's class and race.

II

While the concept of a meritocracy is an ancient one, the word itself is of quite recent vintage. Since it was coined, in 1958,[2] hereditarians have adopted it with delight. As a result, the impression has been created that they are the only ones who believe test scores reflect a meritocracy. Such is not the case. As Eckberg notes, hereditarians and environmentalists "for the most part do not disagree on any of the aspects of the idea of meritocracy. The dispute concerns whether or not the meritocracy is hereditary."[3]

That Eckberg's interpretation is accurate can be determined by analyzing almost any one of a great number of works by environmentalists. As one particularly significant example, let us take *IQ, Heritability and Racism* (1978) by James M. Lawler, a professor of philosophy.[4]

Unusual Reason

Why is James Lawler's book of special significance? Certainly not for the usual reasons, that is, number of copies in circulation and/or recognition-value of its author's name.

Although *IQ, Heritability and Racism* is a book most readers of *The Mismeasure of Man* have never heard of (in fact, its abstruse style precludes a general readership), it has nonetheless attracted the attention of a diverse readership, ranging from the psychometricians themselves to academics in various disciplines to individuals on the left, particularly those influenced by the antitesting protests of the sixties and seventies. The interest of these disparate readers was aroused, albeit for different reasons, by Lawler's definition of his work as a "Marxist critique" of IQ tests.

Apparently as evidence of the validity of this definition, Lawler offers numerous quotations from Marx and Engels. He also paraphrases their views, borrows their terminology to express his own views, and peppers his work with protests against racism, segregation, and apartheid. He does not, however, protest against IQ testing. On the contrary, beneath its radical veneer, *IQ, Heritability and Racism* is one of the most elaborate justifications for the pseudoscience of mental measurement ever published.

In the time, more than a decade, since its publication, there has been no challenge to *IQ, Heritability and Racism*. Those of its readers who accepted it for what it claims to be, not for what it is, may thus react with shock, if not disbelief, to our assertion that it offers a rationale for, not a confrontation with, IQ testing.

"Crucial Question"

As the first step in considering Lawler's thesis, let us look at his comment on meritocracy and the schools: "The crucial question is . . . whether the school systems do in fact select children on the basis of true merit, or whether they essentially reproduce the class differences and racial discrimination that prevail in society at large. This is not a question to which this book can devote any special attention."[5]

It seems odd for a writer to declare a question crucial yet say he will devote no special attention to it—particularly when the question involves class discrimination and racism and he describes his work as a Marxist critique. Despite his disclaimer, however, Lawler *did* devote special attention to the question of whether the schools use IQ tests as a means for selecting children according to merit, or for justifying their prior division by class and race. In fact, it was impossible for him to do otherwise, since his treatment of the tests necessarily provided his answer to the question.

In Lawler's view, IQ tests are "a stage in the development of intelligence theory,"[6] "a historically necessary phase in the history of the science of [human thought]."[7] In accord with his view of the tests as a stage in the development of a science, he set himself the following task: "Our task here will be to try to disentangle the degree of truth captured by the IQ method from the concepts and ideology that are imported into the reality from the consciousness of the mental testers themselves."[8]

Lawler used "truth" and "reality" as synonyms for "intelligence." Thus the task he set himself was to separate the degree of intelligence he believed is "captured" by the IQ method from the concepts and ideology of the mental testers, by which he meant hereditarian concepts and ideology. In so defining his task, he bypassed the question of whether IQ tests do in fact measure intelligence and simply assumed they do what they are claimed to do. At the same time, by identifying IQ testing exclusively with hereditarianism, he overlooked that the "mental testers themselves" are at least as likely to be environmentalists as hereditarians.

If Lawler's definition of his task were read out of context, one would hardly gather that his object was to disentangle IQ testing from hereditarianism. This is not only because he omitted the word, but also because it is an anomaly for an environmentalist to use "reality" as a synonym for "intelligence," since this usage suggests the hereditarian practice of reifying an abstraction. But in using "reality" as he did, Lawler was not in substantive conflict with other environmentalists. They too convert the concept of intelligence into a measurable or testable phenomenon, but— unlike Lawler—do so implicitly.

Theory and Practice

The chapter in *IQ, Heritability and Racism* dealing with IQ history is notable for its omissions. Absent is any mention of such crucial episodes as the WWI army tests and their postwar use to abet passage of the immigration-restriction and eugenic-sterilization laws.

Lawler implicitly justified these omissions by titling his chapter "History of IQ Theory" and also by stating that his overall purpose was to "remov[e] theoretical blinders that operate in much of the literature on IQ."[9] But despite his stated focus on theory, it proved impossible for him to write about IQ history without some reference to the realities of testing. And, inevitably, this led him to suggest, albeit inadvertently, that if mental measurement is "historically necessary," the reasons are far removed from science. For example, he stated that IQ history shows

> an attempt to prove that intelligence is a biologically fixed capacity which is found in different proportions throughout society, so that it can be said that the upper class is innately superior in intelligence to the "lower" classes, and the white colonialists are innately superior in intelligence to the nonwhite races over which they seek to preserve their rule.[10]

Omitting craniometry, Lawler began his treatment of IQ history with Francis Galton (1822–1911), the founder of eugenics and a cousin of Charles Darwin. As Lawler pointed out, Galton attempted to use Darwin's theory of biological evolution to explain social evolution. To support his belief that class and racial hierarchies exist for genetic reasons, he devised tests of sensory reactions, which he assumed to be a measure of intelligence. He dropped his tests when members of the upper class failed to have the more acute reactions to sound, heat, cold, etc., he had anticipated. Lawler wrote, "Despite the failure of the particular tests devised by Galton, certain basic features of his approach continue to be at the foundation of intelligence measurement today. In the first place, a successful test is one whose results confirm judgments *already made* concerning which individuals are more intelligent."[11]

Lawler took note of the a priori nature of IQ testing, but misinterpreted it. The testers' prior judgments are not about "individuals," but about the classes and races they belong to. (Following the mental testers' own practice, Lawler quite often used "individuals" in place of "class" and "race.") Nor do the tests *confirm* judgments already made. If they did, these judgments would be valid, as indeed Lawler considered them to be.

III

While science advances to higher and higher stages, pseudo-science can produce no more than variations on one or another fallacious theme. Because Lawler mistook intelligence measurement for a science, and so saw each successive variation as a progression from one stage to another, he interpreted Binet's method as the "next major step in the development of intelligence tests."[12]

Before considering Lawler's view of the Binet test as a major step, let us look at the test itself.

Mystique and Reality

When Lawler spoke of the IQ test as a "historically necessary stage in the history of the science of [human thought]," he continued the mystification of mental measurement that Binet himself began.

Binet, for example, engaged in mystification when he said his test was designed to "separate natural intelligence and instruction." He continued his mystification by stating, "One might almost say, 'It matters very little what the tests are so long as they are numerous.'"[13] With these pronouncements, Binet created the impression that he selected his test items at random, except that he excluded scholastic-type items.

The opposite is true. Not only did he select his items according to a definite criterion, but that criterion—which he took over from craniology—was school success. According to Chorover,

> [Binet's] basic idea was to design a test . . . on which children at a given age or grade level would do either well or poorly, depending upon whether they were already doing well or poorly in school. Preliminary versions of the test were administered to small groups of children whose scores were compared with their teachers' ratings of classroom performance. In the process, items were deleted or added to

bring about the closest correspondence between test performance and educational age norms. In its final form, Binet's test provided an index of scholastic performance based upon the prevailing standard of scholastic success.[14]

In devising his method, Binet faced a variation of the problem he had encountered as a craniologist, when he had vainly attempted to validate head size as a physical criterion for measuring intelligence by seeking a correlation between it and scholastic performance. Now, with no real criterion to replace the one that had failed him, he could not even attempt to validate his assumption about school performance. It is because he was confronted with this insoluble problem that he mystified his method.

As a primary step in creating the illusion of validity, Binet formulated his test questions so they seemed unrelated to what they were actually based upon, the school curriculum. He also introduced mystifying terminology, as, for example, when he declared that a child's score on the intelligence scale represented his or her "mental level," or, as it soon came to be called, "mental age." (Although there is a technical difference in the way it is calculated, an IQ, or "intelligence quotient," is the conceptual equivalent of mental age.)

What this terminology concealed is that the normal mental level for each age group was determined by that group's average test score, which corresponded to the average school performance for the group. Thus the relationship of a child's score to the average score determined whether he or she would be classified as of average, superior, or inferior intelligence. This meant that, contrary to the claims made for it, the test did not rank individuals in an objective way but according to an arbitrary standard. Because the test was constructed with scholastic-type items, the children from groups whose education was superior necessarily made the higher scores—which upheld the prior assumption that different classes and races have superior and inferior intelligence.

Binet could hardly have been unaware that he had devised a circular method in which the assumption that school success is a measure of intelligence is "validated" by a test whose covert criterion is school success. That he was troubled by this point is the only way to explain his proposal that head measurement be used to "confirm" the verdicts of mental measurement.

IV

In returning to Lawler, we find that he held Binet took a major step because he "broke" from Galton's use of a physical standard[15] and because he "refined" Galton's "principle of measuring intelligence of people in general by establishing their abilities relative to each other"[16]—which means, when demystified, that Binet did not rank test takers into a single group, as Galton did, but separated them into age groups and ranked the members of each group according to the average score for that age. Lawler accepted this as a "relative" method of measuring intelligence but also believed it should be improved upon. To this end, he proposed yet another revised version of the IQ test.[17]

It seems contradictory that Lawler accepted the Binet test as a measure of intelligence since he made certain admissions about it, e.g., that there was no objective standard for validating it and that its items were selected to conform to a standard of school success. What explains this apparent contrariety is that, as an environmentalist, Lawler believed a group's level of intelligence correlates with its level of education.

Lawler—apparently unaware that Binet himself made the classic hereditarian claim that his test was designed to "separate natural intelligence from instruction"—stated that Binet's test was "subject to ideological interpretations quite alien to his own."[18] Thus he suggested that IQ tests—which rank classes and races in a way that corresponds to their ranking in the social hierarchy—are dangerous instruments only when interpreted from a hereditarian standpoint.

"Far-Reaching Conclusions"

From Binet, Lawler moved to Terman. Although he described Terman as "the founder of the most important mental test,"[19] he was concerned about Terman's hereditarian views. Thus, after quoting Terman's remarks on the tests of African-Americans and the minorities in the Southwest, he wrote, "Gone is the purely pragmatic approach of Binet, who saw his tests as practical instruments for identifying children who needed special attention in order to overcome their educational deficiencies. Instead there is the identification of a . . . veritable racial caste of manual laborers."[20]

Here Lawler made the environmentalist's traditional contrast between Binet and Terman, suggesting that one used his test for a benign and the other for a malignant purpose. First, while his remarks on Terman were certainly accurate in an overall way, they did not quite describe the way Terman used his test: rather than say he used it to identify a virtual racial caste of laborers, it would be more accurate to say he used it to justify the status of those who had long been so identified.

Nor did Binet use his test for identification purposes. There was no need for him to identify children with scholastic difficulties, since these children had already been so identified by their grades. Again, Binet used his test for a far-from-benign purpose: to identify inferior intelligence, not inferior schooling, as the source of the children's scholastic problems.

Continuing, Lawler wrote, "Perhaps, one might suppose, there has been some additional feature which Terman introduced into Binet's tests that might have partially excused his drawing such far-reaching conclusions as to the mental capabilities of the most exploited and abused sectors of the U.S. population."[21] Lawler did not believe Terman introduced any test feature that might have "partially excused" his coming to "such far-reaching" or hereditarian conclusions. Of course, one might consider it far-reaching to conclude that minority groups are of inferior intelligence for *any* reason. Lawler's objective, however, was not to contest the IQ test's verdict but to establish his own interpretation of it. Where Terman contended that these minorities are fit for no more than manual labor because of a genetic deficiency in intelligence, Lawler turned matters around by suggesting they have been rendered deficient in intelligence by exploitation.

While his radical-sounding thesis (he used "most exploited" where other environmentalists would say "poorest") appears to condemn the relegation of certain racial and ethnic groups to society's bottom rungs, it actually does the opposite: by correlating a group's level of intelligence with its social level, it provides yet another rationale for the social status quo.

The Surrogate Stratagem

I

"The validity of intelligence tests is hardly a question that the psychologist would care to debate with Mr. Lippmann," declared Terman during their encounter.[1]

Not only are psychometricians today still averse to debating this question, but they still justify their resistance on the grounds that mental measurement is a science beyond the comprehension of any but experts like themselves. As Banesh Hoffmann, the mathematician and test critic, observed, when the testers are challenged they "grow arrogant, claim to be scientific, and use their statistics as a smokescreen."[2]

The testers display their arrogance not only by putting down test critics, but also in other ways. For example, they arrogantly redefine such key words as "intelligence."[3] The best known or, depending on one's outlook, most notorious example of this was provided by Edmund Boring, a Harvard psychologist and early tester, when he issued a circular dictum: "Intelligence as a measurable capacity must at the start be defined as the capacity to do well in an intelligence test. Intelligence is what the tests test."[4]

When the testers use the redefinition ploy to parry charges that intelligence tests do not measure intelligence, they get caught in another bind. They insist that they eschew the ordinary definition of intelligence, but they must also sustain the illusion that the tests measure what is ordinarily meant by "intelligence." Chorover noted:

> Whereas psychometricians may insist that there is a special or proper way to understand their definitions, the actual fact is that they define intelligence in the same way everyone else does. They use the terms *intelligence* and *IQ* as synonyms for *brightness, smartness, cleverness, mental ability,* and so forth. And they do so in ways clearly calculated to transfer to IQ scores the conceptual, evaluative, emotional, and subjective connotations that are normally evoked when someone is called "smart" or "stupid."[5]

The Conversion

When Boring asserted that "intelligence as a measurable capacity" must be defined as the "capacity to do well in an intelligence test," he, as the testers still do, obscured the distinction between making a higher score on an IQ test and having the capacity, or potential, for making one. But since capacity, like intelligence, is a nonmeasurable trait, he also provided an early example of another of the testers' dilemmas: how to sustain the illusion that intelligence tests measure intelligence when in fact they measure or test the IQ method's *surrogates* for intelligence, namely, the skills, information, and social values called for by the test questions.

In a comment on the types of items used in IQ tests, Lawler provided, albeit inadvertently, something of a description of the way in which the testers make it appear that they are measuring a child's intelligence, when in fact they are measuring the degree to which the child has acquired the surrogates for intelligence: "One justification given for such a variety of items is that 'intelligence' is assumed to be a highly complex function, and so is measured by testing various abilities, information, and what seems to be just plain opinion."[6]

Lawler's conversion of "intelligence" from a *concept* to a *function* was in itself a curious step. From the standpoint of psychometrics, however, it was an obligatory one, because a concept cannot be measured, but a function—or, rather, the performance of a function—*can* be measured or tested. Thus, one may infer from Lawler's remarks, the IQ method requires children to perform designated functions, and takes their performance of these functions as the measure of their intelligence.

As Lawler put it, IQ tests test abilities, information, and "just plain opinion." In reality, while the tests do involve information and opinion (or dominant social values), they do not test abilities—that is, not if "abilities" is interpreted, as it usually is, to mean "capacities" or "potentialities." That the testers do use abilities in this sense is illustrated by their alternative definitions of IQ tests, i.e., as tests of "intelligence" or of "abilities." Of course, abilities can also be interpreted to mean "skills." This ambiguity allows the testers to have it the other way around; when under fire, they can insist that they mean for the tests to be interpreted as no more than a measure of skills.

Although Lawler did not attribute the "justification" for constructing IQ tests with a variety of items to any source, it can be traced to Binet's dictum that intelligence tests should be comprised of numerous items. In any event, by his mystifying presentation of the justification, Lawler obscured the reason for so constructing the tests: while a test with many items can no more measure intelligence than a test with just a few, it can do more to create the illusion it does what it is claimed to do.

II

The criticism that has done the most to expose the IQ tests' invalidity is the one most frequently leveled: test bias. To counter this charge, the testers use a variety of techniques, including one analogous to that they use with "intelligence."

According to the Committee on Ability Testing, when the specialist and the nonspecialist talk about bias in tests, they "often talk right past each other."[7] Not really. When the testers say a test is not biased, they clearly attempt to create the impression the test is not biased in the usual sense, and only when pressed do they claim to be speaking in a strictly technical sense, i.e., to be using the statistical definition of bias, which has nothing to do with bias in the sense of racial and class discrimination.[8]

When the testers talked of bias, presumably they did not talk right past Hoffmann. But instead of accepting the special definition of a nonbiased test as proof that IQ tests are not biased, the mathematician declared, "We shouldn't have to persuade anyone these days that IQ tests cannot possibly measure anything that can legitimately be called intelligence. These tests are clearly culturally biased."[9]

Hoffmann also said, "I think that the inherent bias in the IQ test is a good reason for not using it."[10]

The tests' inherent bias—inherent because their underlying standard, school success, is subjective or arbitrary—presents special problems for those who attempt to reconcile liberal or radical social concerns with support for mental testing. Lawler, for example, not only criticized those items that are obviously culturally biased, but also acknowledged that *all* IQ tests are biased.[11] Yet he also insisted that IQ tests are "not totally arbitrary."[12] The arbitrary items, he indicated, are those involving values, while the nonarbitrary ones are of the scholastic type or, as he put it, those "involving general scholastic ability."[13] In other words, he made the circular suggestion that to do well on items requiring scholastic skills, a child must have general scholastic ability—a hypothetical trait that sounds a good deal like what hereditarians call "general intelligence."

Gould is also among those writers who defend certain categories of items against the bias charge. Discussing the WWI Alpha, he criticized the blatantly biased items (those calling for a knowledge of such matters as brand names and baseball players).

But he was ambiguous, not to say dismissive, of bias in those items (such as analogies) that implicitly require scholastic skills: "These familiar parts are not especially subject to charges of cultural bias, at least no more so than their modern descendants."[14]

From these remarks, one may get the impression not only that the blatantly biased items have no modern descendents, but also that certain types of items are not especially or really biased. But if certain kinds of items have been somewhat less vulnerable to charges of bias, it is only because their bias is concealed rather than overt.

Coordinated Biases

From a functional standpoint there is no distinction between crassly biased IQ-test items and those that appear to be non-biased. Because *all* types of test items are biased (if not explicitly, then implicitly, or in some combination thereof), and because the tests' racial and class biases correspond to the society's, each element of a test plays its part in ranking children in the way their respective groups are ranked in the social order.

Take words. They serve as a social sorting device because test items in general, as well as vocabulary subtests, sentence-completion items, etc., in particular, use words that are more familiar to the white middle-class test takers than to the other groups. Then there is the tests' use of information that is also more accessible to the same children. For instance, the Weschler Intelligence Scale for Children (WISC) calls for information on subjects ranging from English weights and measures to literature, history, geography, and biology.

There is also the use of contexts—for analogies, math problems, etc.—that are more familiar to white than to black children, or to boys than to girls. Further, new research shows that the use of men rather than women in test items and the projection of women in stereotyped roles has an adverse effect on girls' scores.[15] Obviously this finding also has significant implications for African-American, Latino, and other minority test takers.

In the *NAACP Report on Minority Testing* (1976), Buell G. Gallagher commented on the use of words and subject matter for discriminating along racial and class lines:

> I once watched two persons taking the same test . . . . They showed startling differences: one ranked very high, the other quite low. The reason was not hard to find: they came from opposite sides of the tracks. The test items were things which had been part of the intimate daily life of one, while the other had never seen and seldom heard of the items mentioned in the test.[16]

To fail an IQ-test item, a child need not be absolutely unfamiliar with it but only relatively so, since speed is a requirement. The WISC picture-completion subtest, for example, allows just fifteen seconds for naming or pointing to the missing part of a picture.

A more obvious form of bias appears in the items involving values. The prototype for these appeared in the original Stanford Binet, which asked fourteen-year-olds to explain the following:

> My neighbor has been having queer visitors. First a doctor came to his house, then a lawyer, then a minister (preacher or priest). What do you think happened there?

The correct answer was, "The doctor came to attend a sick person, the lawyer to make his will, and the minister to preach his funeral."[17] Making it clear that even the slightest deviation from conformity is a mark of low intelligence, Terman failed this answer: "Somebody was sick; the lawyer wanted his money."[18]

Although the testers offer a variety of rationales for including different types of items, they say as little as possible about those involving values, hoping, perhaps, that their silence will be interpreted to mean these items play so insignificant a role as to need no comment. In reality, to earn a score on many items in contemporary tests, a child must express agreement with prevailing values. Amado M. Padilla, a psychology professor, and Blas M. Garza, a school principal, observe,

The values underlying many of the test items . . . are outside the life experience of some children. One item on the Stanford-Binet subtest for ten-year olds requires that the child give two reasons . . . why "most people would rather have an automobile than a bicycle." Similarly, on the WISC General Comprehension subtest, we find such questions as . . . "Why is it better to pay bills by check than by cash?" "Why is it generally better to give money to an organized charity than it is to a street beggar?" : . . Many Mexican-American or Puerto Rican children may be unable to respond to such questions because their life experiences have contributed to the formation of a different set of values. . . . [A] child whose family lives on the fringe of poverty may have little idea of the values associated with checking accounts or donating to organized charities.[19]

In defending their tests against the bias charge, the test makers occasionally concede that a particular item is biased, while also insisting that it is an anomaly. If they deem it advisable to cite a biased item, they are likely to choose one that calls for, say, a knowledge of instruments in a symphony orchestra. Not only do they avoid comment on the type cited by Garza and Padilla, but also on items that are explicitly racist and/or sexist.

In an analysis of test questions, the editors of *Principal* provided examples of racist items, including the following:

When a dove begins to associate with crows, its feathers remain _____, but its heart grows black.
F black   **G** white   **H** dirty   **J** spread   **K** good

"Not only is the statement itself erroneous, but think of the emotional impact of an item like this on a black child," the editors commented.[20] And one might add: Think also of the impact of such an item on a white child.

The editors also provided this example of an overtly biased item:

The pictures in the box go together in a certain way. We say: "Boy is to trousers as girl is to what?"

[The pictures in the box are of a white boy and girl and of a pair of pants. The answer is to be chosen from adjoining pictures of a dress, a roller skate, a bicycle, and a white doll.]

To earn a score on this analogy (whose all-white illustrations conform to the testers' notion of an environmental norm), a child must accept an inaccurate, sexist premise. As the editors pointed out, "Most little girls wear blue jeans these days as often as they wear dresses."[21]

The editors also offered an example of the ambiguity and the notion of morality to be found in the tests:

You can't _____ him, he was just doing his job.
   R annoy   **S** help   **T** blame   **U** find   **V** trust

"The answer wanted is 'blame,' an excuse made famous by legions of low-level Nazis during the Nuremberg trials," observed the editors.[22]

The editors' analysis appeared in *The Myth of Measurability*, a collection of articles from *Principal*. Examples of crassly biased, as well as illogical, ambiguous, and inaccurate items were also presented in other articles. "Lest you be tempted to conclude that the authors have deliberately selected the most outrageous examples from the tests, we urge you to take the time to examine the major tests in their entirety," stated Paul L. Houts, editor of *Principal*.[23]

Covert Bias

To sustain the illusion that IQ tests are not arbitrary, or biased, the testers do not limit themselves to direct denials or to insisting that certain items, whose bias is so blatant that even they cannot deny it, are mere anomalies. Above all, they depend on mystification—as, for example, when they classify items such as analogies, which call for the skills of formal logic, as tests of "reasoning ability."

By so classifying these items, the testers blur the distinction between the skills of formal logic, which are acquired in school, and the human power of logical analysis, which develops in the totality of life situations. In this way, they create the impression that children from groups whose education is inferior, and who thus do not have the requisite skills, are children who lack the ability to reason.

The tests' falsity is also revealed by the testers' assumption that analogy items can have only one right answer. "[A]n analogy question never has a unique answer," pointed out Judah L. Schwartz, a professor of engineering science and education, who demonstrated that one or more alternative answers can be justified for any analogy, whether verbal, visual, or numerical.[24]

Thus, as one delves further and further into test construction, one finds a maze of arbitrary steps taken to ensure that the items selected — the surrogates for intelligence — will rank children of different classes and races in conformity with a mental hierarchy that is presupposed to exist.

The Other
Side of the Tracks

I

Although IQ tests are claimed to perform a variety of functions, their real function is unvarying; they place children on scholastic tracks that correlate with the proverbial side of the tracks the children live on. The tests' vaunted versatility is thus not based on what they actually do, but rather upon the fact that their single function can be defined in a variety of ways and performed in many contexts.

As an example of the latter point, take the post-WWI period, when the tests were first put into general use in the schools. Not coincidentally, it was a time when high-school education, which had been highly restricted along the lines of class, race, and nationality, was becoming far more widely available, albeit at a far lower rate for blacks than for whites. With the tests, relatively affluent children could be steered to an academic high-school education, as they had been on an *overtly* class basis in the pretesting era, while whites from blue-collar backgrounds could be steered to vocational programs in the same high schools or to separate vocational high schools. At the same time, the tests justified segregated, inferior education at all levels for blacks.

The use of the tests for steering students from different groups to different programs in the same school was repeated in a different and more dramatic context after the Supreme Court's 1954 order on school desegregation. Although many school systems resisted this decision overtly, many others did so covertly. The favored means of noncompliance in the latter cases were IQ and IQ-type tests; with the tests, African-American children could be diverted to a separate and unequal education in supposedly desegregated schools. Offering the psychometricians' interpretation of this phenomenon, the Committee on Ability Testing stated, "Many formerly segregated school systems introduced testing programs to track students into ability groups with the effect of continuing patterns of racial segregation within school buildings."[1]

The claim that testing-tracking programs have the "effect" of resegregating blacks—i.e., that segregation in schools with such programs is merely an unavoidable by-product of guiding children according to their ability—has encountered successful legal challenges in some instances. For example, in 1967 U.S. Circuit Court Judge Skelly Wright, ruling in a case (*Hobson v. Hansen*) brought against the Washington, D.C., school system, held that the tests that allegedly measure ability and the tracks that supposedly provide an education based on individual differences in ability, actually maintain unequal education on both racial and class lines—thereby helping to keep black and working-class children locked into the social and economic status of the groups they come from. Barring the Washington schools— which operated a four-track system—from tracking, Judge Wright declared, "Even in concept the track system is undemocratic and discriminatory."[2]

To circumvent rulings such as this, schools have made legal appeals, substituted different tests to perform the tracking function, or used the same tests in an allegedly different manner.

Selma and the Track System

More than two decades later, the nation's schools were functioning as if Judge Wright's landmark decision against tracking did
not exist. But anti-tracking sentiment across the country had
grown significantly. And in 1990, an unusual set of circumstances put tracking in the spotlight.

In Selma, Alabama, at the end of 1989, a white-majority school
board refused to renew the contract of the city's first African-
American superintendent of schools, who had taken measures
to counteract the resegregation that followed the official desegregation of the city's schools. The action of these board members
set off protests in early 1990—the year marking the twenty-fifth
anniversary of a historic Selma event: "Bloody Sunday," when a
civil-rights march led by Martin Luther King, Jr. was assaulted
by state troopers and sheriff's deputies. With the media focusing
on Selma for the anniversary, the issue underlying the new
Selma protests—tracking—was aired nationally.

"Before the 60's we had separate and segregated schools, and
then came this tracking, which was a way of students walking
through the same school doors and getting segregated once they
got inside," declared Hank Sanders, an Alabama state senator.[3]

The superintendent, Norward Roussell, was not in a position
to do away with the track system, but he took steps that opened
up academic education to more blacks. Nevertheless, segregation
remained solidly in place. And segregation will remain in place
in Selma or anywhere else that tracking—by IQ or other standardized tests, or by any other means—continues.[4]

II

When children are placed on a lower track, there is little likelihood they will ever get off. The quality of the instruction, the
nature of the courses, and the time allocated to learning activities are far inferior to what is provided for children on higher
tracks.

It is obvious that biological determinists, whose views prevailed at the time tracking was introduced, would expect children placed on lower tracks to stay there. But what may be less obvious is that environmentalism, which is portrayed as a hopeful thesis, leads to the same expectation. In fact, environmentalists have produced many rationales for tracking. Among the more explicit of these was presented by Lawler.

In an approach that brought him into direct conflict with Judge Wright's findings that "even in concept" tracking is "undemocratic and discriminatory," Lawler denied that these characteristics are inherent in tracking. Maintaining that tracking acquires these features only when practiced in one form rather than another, he writes, "The existence of a basically segregated school system in the United States constitutes a national tracking system in which race, and not IQ, is clearly of primary importance."[5]

By interpreting segregation in separate schools as a form of tracking in which "race, and not IQ," is of "primary importance," Lawler attempted to make a substantive distinction between tracking by race and tracking by IQ tests. In other words, he overlooked that IQ tests are racially biased devices that resegregate African-American children within nominally desegregated schools. Thus his position was compatible with that of those who contend that if the testing-tracking system resegregates, it is only as a by-product of sorting children according to their intelligence/abilities.

"Speaking Personally"

In turning to Gould, we find that he too is among the many environmentalists who offer rationales for tracking. For example, when he insisted that Binet's test should have been used "consistently as he intended" — that is, for assigning children to classes for the mentally retarded — Gould was endorsing the use of IQ tests for assigning children to the lowest rung of the track system, EMR classes.

He also lent support to the track system by approving a related, although not identical, practice, that is, the use of the tests to classify children "learning disabled." Unexpectedly stepping from his role as author into the role of author-as-parent, he spoke of this practice in both a highly favorable and a highly confusing way: "Ironically, many American school boards have come full cycle, and now use IQ tests only as Binet originally recommended: as instruments for assessing children with specific learning problems. Speaking personally, I feel that tests of the IQ type were helpful in the proper diagnosis of my own learning-disabled son."[6]

Why, one may ask, did Gould say that many school boards *now* use the tests as Binet originally intended, when in fact they have long used them to classify children mentally retarded? The answer is that only by revising Binet's recommendation—i.e., substituting "learning disabled," a category that did not exist in Binet's time, for "mentally retarded"—could he introduce the question of his son.

To assess Gould's remarks, one should be aware that a child may be classified learning disabled if there is a "disparity" between the child's IQ-test score and his or her school performance. This procedure—which implicitly treats IQ tests as a measure of "innate" intelligence—is in effect in forty-nine states.

According to Gould, IQ-type tests helped diagnose his son's condition. The tests, however, are not diagnostic instruments. They are simply devices that produce scores that lend themselves to one or another interpretation. If a child is of higher socioeconomic status, an IQ test will not be expected to substitute for comprehensive medical and psychological examinations.

Gould did not identify his son's learning disability, let alone say that a learning disability may be defined as anything from a specific physical problem to something as ambiguous as "attention deficits." In any event, being classified learning disabled carries no stigma for children of higher socioeconomic status; in fact, such children will often be described as "above average" in intelligence. They will also be provided with tutors or sent to private schools that specialize in teaching learning-disabled children. Children in ordinary middle-class circumstances are, however, likely to face great difficulties in obtaining proper instruction. And so far as children of lower socioeconomic status are concerned, being classified learning disabled will more than likely mean consignment to an EMR class—with IQ tests serving as the justification.

If a child of lower social status is diagnosed as having, say, attention deficits, there is little likelihood that an effort will be made to see whether there is a physical basis for the child's behavior. On the other hand, if none exists, other questions arise. Why should attention deficits—or, properly speaking, lack of attention in class—imply something is wrong with the child? Why should it not suggest something is wrong with the school?

That the school authorities shun such a diagnosis indicates that the learning-disability thesis is yet another means for carrying out what Richard H. de Lone calls the "systematic misclassification of black children as retarded."[7] De Lone, author of *Small Futures* (1977), writes,

> [T]he categories by which children are classified are often fuzzy, and diagnosis may rely entirely or partly on observed behavior rather than on any demonstrated organic or neurological problem. This is especially true in the burgeoning new field of learning disabilities. For instance, according to the President's Committee on Mental Retardation [1976], about 90 percent of all children diagnosed as retarded have no known organic difficulty but suffer from so-called socioeconomic retardation.[8]

Thus the environmentalist tenet that lower socioeconomic status produces mental inferiority was the quasi-official justification for classifying children mentally retarded in the period in question. However, as is evident from Jensen's article in 1969, the genetic thesis played a significant, albeit officially unacknowledged, role in the same period for so classifying children.

III

A striking example of the steps taken to maintain the "systematic misclassification" of black children as mentally retarded can be found in a recommendation made by the Committee on Ability Testing. In a critique of the defense in *Larry P. v. Riles*, the committee stated:

> Had the defendants presented convincing evidence that there is in fact more mild mental retardation among black students, they might have rebutted the prima facie case, as indeed they could have by showing that the tests in question had been validated for the specific use on the specific population. But nothing in the evidence convinced the court that the tests were not culturally biased against black students.[9]

Having assumed that its readers, the "decision makers," would take its claim of more mental retardation among African-American children as a given, the committee also expected them to accept its proposal that in future trials school officials should be prepared to show that IQ tests, as the means for assigning black children to EMR classes in disproportionate numbers, are not biased against black students because they have been validated for use on them.

Let us look at the test makers' validation criteria and the role assigned them in countering charges of bias.

"Validating" the Tests

Basically, four validation criteria are applied to IQ tests: *face validity, concurrent validity, predictive validity,* and *construct validity.*

Face validity. If, in the view of test specialists, a test appears to do what it is claimed to do, it is said to have face validity. This procedure is highly important to the test makers for commercial reasons; a test must "look valid" to prospective buyers. And, transparent a device as it is, it plays a role—even in court—in defending the tests against the bias charge. Test defenders use face validity to argue that if there is any bias in a test, it is restricted to a small number of items, i.e., to those items whose bias is so obvious it cannot be denied.[10]

Concurrent validity. A test whose results correlate with other tests of its kind is said to have concurrent validity. In other words, this criterion validates a newer test by assuming the validity of one or another of its predecessors.

Predictive validity. When the testers say a test has predictive validity, they claim it is not biased. Underlying this claim is the substitution (covertly when possible) of the statistical definition of bias for the ordinary one. According to the Committee on Ability Testing, "Precise use would restrict the term 'test bias' to systematic differences in the predictive power of tests related to group identity."[11] Thus if there are no systematic differences between the predictions of an intelligence/ability test and the scholastic performances of the groups in question—that is, if prediction correlates with performance to the same degree for each group—the test is said to have predictive validity.

It is, of course, hardly surprising that a group's performance on a test that is biased either for or against that group would correlate with the group's performance in schools that have the same biases as the tests. But the fact that such statistically precise correlations can be achieved—thus qualifying the test for unbiased status—may seem a bit surprising. Judah Schwartz pointed to the explanation:

> [W]hy is it that group ability tests predict school achievement as well as they do? The answer is quite simple. Group achievement tests and group ability tests are sufficiently similar that without labels, one has difficulty telling which is which. If these group ability tests are used to predict, and group achievement tests are used to confirm those predictions, why should anyone be surprised?[12]

Construct validity. Construct validation carries the mystification of mental measurement to its outer limits. In fact, it is so mystifying, not to say nebulous, that the psychometricians themselves appear to have difficulty describing it. As the Committee on Ability Testing put it, "Construct validation is addressed to the question of what it is that ability tests measure."[13] It seems surprising that, after all these years, the testers would do an about-face and question what it is the tests measure. In reality, of course, they do not. Instead they use construct validation for another, familiar, purpose: to sustain the illusion that the tests measure what they are claimed to measure.

With construct validation, the testers adduce arguments and statistical data to support their claims for a test. This effort centers upon "factor analysis," an abstruse mathematical process that is used to determine the degree of correlation between a test and its subtests, the test and its individual items, and the test and other tests. Although the existence of the correlations proves nothing about their cause, the testers claim the factor accounting for the correlations is the hypothesized trait the test is alleged to measure, e.g., intelligence or ability.

The real reason for the correlations between tests, test items, etc., is not difficult to find, because they are a condition of test construction. "Tests that had low correlation with the total were dropped," acknowledged Terman.[14]

In his critique of *The Mismeasure of Man*, Lewontin delved into the question of the correlations.

> A chief selling point of new tests, as announced in their advertising, is their excellent agreement with the original Stanford-Binet test. They have been carefully cut to fit.
>
> Moreover, the agreement of the results of various parts of the same tests has also been built into them. In order for the original Stanford-Binet to have won credibility as an *intelligence* test, it necessarily had to order children in conformity with the *a priori* judgment of psychologists and teachers about what they thought intelligence consisted of.

No one will use an "intelligence" test that gives highest marks to those children everyone "knows" to be stupid. During the construction of the tests, questions that were poorly correlated with others were dropped, since they clearly did not measure "intelligence," until a maximally consistent set was found.[15]

IV

"Causal reasons lie behind the positive correlations of most mental tests. But what reasons?" asked Gould.[16] Although the answer, as Lewontin (not to say Terman) made evident, lies in the construction of the tests, Gould did not discuss test construction.

Instead of taking note of such mundane matters as the dropping of test items that do not produce the desired correlations, Gould offered a mystifying presentation of the debate between two early psychometricians, Charles Spearman and L.L. Thurstone, over the cause of the correlations. What makes Gould's presentation so mystifying is that it revolved around a lengthy discourse on factor analysis.

Why in a book aimed at a general readership did he offer a dissertation on this highly technical subject? It is impossible, he suggested, to understand the history of mental measurement or its contemporary rationale without understanding factor analysis.[17] If this contention is correct, those readers who lack what is a virtual requirement for penetrating his dissertation—a background in mathematics—will have to do what they are so often told: leave matters pertaining to mental testing to the mental testers.

So far as understanding mental measurement is concerned, all one actually need know about factor analysis is the role it plays in mystifying this pseudoscience. "The very complexity of the statistical manipulation is part of the mystique of intelligence testing, validating it by making it inaccessible to nonexperts," noted Lewontin.[18]

"In the Absence of Evidence"

The issue in the Spearman-Thurstone debate, which the mental-testing establishment invests with vast significance, was how intelligence should be defined. Spearman, a British hereditarian, assumed that "general intelligence" (*g*) underlies the correlations, and he used factor analysis to uphold his assumption. Thurstone, an American hereditarian, assumed that "primary mental abilities" (PMA's) are the cause of the correlations, and used factor analysis to uphold his assumption. The reason for the variation in their respective results is quite simple; each used a variation of factor analysis designed to produce the desired outcome.

In discussing their argument, Gould stated that there is no biological evidence for either man's contention. He pointed out that *g*, which Spearman regarded as a biological entity, is merely a line or axis known in factor analysis as the "first principal component"; when Thurstone's form of factor analysis is used, it disappears. Gould also pointed out that Thurstone too was guilty of reification, and that he "dethroned *g* not by being right with his alternate system, but by being equally wrong."[19]

Although Gould presented more than enough evidence for rejecting both the Spearman and Thurstone positions, he did not do so. Instead he identified with one:

> In the absence of corroborative evidence from biology for one scheme or the other, how can one decide? Ultimately, however much a scientist hates to admit it, the decision becomes a matter of taste, or of prior preference based on personal or cultural biases. Spearman and Burt, as privileged citizens of class-conscious Britain, defended *g* and its linear ranking. Thurstone preferred individual profiles and numerous primary abilities.[20]

Thus Gould created an artificial dilemma in which a scientist—instead of being free to reject both uncorroborated schemes—is compelled to select one. And since Gould acknowledged that the choice cannot be made on scientific grounds, he suggested it be made on social ones. But a social choice between the two schemes is as baseless as a scientific one; in reality, the choice is simply one between different methods of scoring IQ tests.

Spearman, in keeping with his view that general intelligence underlies the correlations, preferred a single score, the IQ. Thurstone, in keeping with his view that primary mental abilities account for the correlations, preferred that scores be recorded for the subtests, the results constituting "individual profiles." Thurstone's approach is the prototype for Gould's view that intelligence should be measured as multiple quantities rather than as a single one. That Gould, as an environmentalist, is a current champion of a thesis devised by a hereditarian is another illustration of how almost any claim associated with IQ testing is adaptable to either point of view.

In associating linear ranking, or ranking according to a single score, with "privileged citizens of class-conscious Britain," Gould suggested Thurstone's method is more democratic. But class- and race-biased tests will rank test takers according to their class and race whichever way they are scored. That there may be variations in an individual's subtest scores (test correlations are based on *group* averages and vary considerably in strength) does not change the fact that an individual with a lower overall score will have subtest scores that are lower in more instances, if not in every instance, than an individual with a higher overall score. Nor does it change the fact that the scoring *level* for the various subtests will be higher or lower for individuals as a whole according to their class and race. Further, some subtests are invested with more importance than others, and this differentiation also works in favor of those whose status is superior by virtue of class, race, and/or sex.

By associating class distinctions only with Britain, Gould brings to mind Lewontin's observation that in the United States "the reality of social class" is "firmly denied." The firm denial is, of course, accompanied by equally firm, not to say rigid, steps to preserve class and racial divisions—as demonstrated by the testing-tracking operation.

V

Far from signifying test validity, the intricate test correlations are a sign of the test makers' power to manipulate their products. As Chorover pointed out, "[I]t is a fairly simple matter to manipulate a test in order to produce almost any desired result . . . . [T]est makers can and do manipulate their tests in order to make the results conform with prevailing social and scholastic standards."[21]

While official tests are manipulated to conform to prevailing standards, other tests have been constructed that conflict with these standards. For example, tests have been devised on which the standard racial bias is reversed, so that blacks outscore whites. These tests have helped demystify the pseudoscience of mental measurement by making it clear that the direction of a test's bias—shaped in these instances by the selection of items more familiar to blacks than to whites—determines the test's outcome.

For an example of the way in which official tests are manipulated, let us take the Stanford-Binet. On the original version, girls outscored boys by a few points. On a revised version, this embarrassing differential was eliminated. Terman located those test parts on which girls scored higher than boys and vice versa and made substitutions that brought about equivalent scores.

But why, it may be asked, did not Terman—given his social-Darwinist outlook—design a test to support the claim that women are inferior in intelligence? The answer is not to be found in his views, which were adjustable within certain limits, but in what his test was designed to do, i.e., justify the prevailing standards, which called for girls and boys to be placed on the same general academic tracks. If his test had instead been constructed to uphold the allegation that girls have less "general intelligence" than boys, girls could not have been placed on the same tracks as boys without threatening the test's credibility as a means for justifying racial segregation and tracking according to class.

Since the scoring differentials on certain subtests are balanced out so as to achieve gender parity in overall scores, the subtest disparities may seem innocuous. They are not. Although they are an outcome of pressure on boys and girls to pursue interests in keeping with traditional sex roles, they are interpreted to mean that girls are deficient in the abilities required for certain careers, especially scientific ones. As the children grow older, these social pressures not only become stronger in general but are reinforced in particular by the schools, which treat boys as better suited to math than girls.

Manipulating the SAT

By the time students take the SAT, the gender scoring differentials have predictably become more pronounced. Selected subtests are not weighted to equalize those differentials, as was the case when girls outscored boys on the Stanford-Binet. On the contrary, the SAT has been weighted to widen a gender scoring differential that from the start favored males.

Since the SAT was introduced in 1926, men have scored higher on it than women. But the gender gap, which was primarily due to men's higher scores on the math subtest, was partially offset until 1972 by women's higher scores on the verbal subtest. After that date, men began to do better than women on this subtest; by 1986, they scored significantly higher on it than women. ETS offered a strange explanation: it had changed the verbal test to create a "better balance for the scores between the sexes."[22] What ETS had done was add questions whose contexts favored men and eliminate those whose contexts favored women.

These are the findings of Phyllis Rosser, who has published a comprehensive study of the SAT and sex bias, *The SAT Gender Gap* (1989). The test's gender bias applies to women at each socioeconomic level and from every racial and ethnic background. The test's biases doubly penalize African-American, Latino, and other minority women and add a third penalty for lower socioeconomic status.

Studies of women's performance on other math tests have raised questions about the gender differential on the SAT math tests. "[W]hen math content is made relevant to female experience, males do not outperform females on math problems."[23] The SAT math questions that produced the biggest gender gap called for computing a basketball team's won/lost record.

Women's scores are lower on the SAT despite the fact that their grade-point averages in high school are higher than men's, including in math. (Given the discouragement girls face when it comes to math, the latter point is particularly significant.) A study in 1988 of four thousand high-school students in one county showed that girls who took the same advanced classes as boys in calculus, pre-calculus, and algebra made higher math grades than boys but lower scores on the SAT math test.[24]

Women also make lower scores on the other major college entrance exam, the American College Test. Because of the ACT and SAT's sex bias, women have been deprived of scholarships (two-thirds of the National Merit Scholarship Awards have gone to men) and acceptance by the colleges of their choice.

Girls' scores have also been consistently higher than boys' on the major standardized tests in high school. But now two studies show scoring deficits for young women, similar to their scoring deficits on the SAT, on certain high-school achievement tests. The studies—one of which was conducted by the National Assessment of Educational Progress (NAEP)—revealed a familiar, circular pattern. They "used tests written by ETS and these findings are often cited by ETS researchers to justify the gender gap on the SAT."[25] The studies, Rosser stresses, "raise questions about political intent."[26]

The testers provide their standard rationale for using the SAT: to predict scholastic performance. But the disparity between the testers' stated intentions and their real ones is nowhere more clearly revealed than with the SAT. That test consistently *under-*

predicts first-year college performance for women and *overpre-dicts* for men—thus violating one of the testers' own, specially designed standards of validity. Obviously, in the testers' opinion this is no reason for abandoning a test whose role is analogous to that of IQ tests; it helps keep academic barriers in place for those groups historically confronted by them.[27]

Myth into Method

The Committee on Ability Testing was "convened at a time of widespread controversy about the use of standardized tests to assess individual differences."[1]

Thus the authors of *Ability Testing* alluded to the controversy between those who claim standardized tests are used to assess individual differences—that is, discriminate among individuals on the basis of their intelligence, ability, aptitude, etc.—and those who charge the tests are used to discriminate among individuals on the basis of their class and race. As a work dedicated to upholding the testers' side of the controversy, *Ability Testing* has a great many antecedents. The most immediate of these is *Bias in Mental Testing* (1980), by Jensen.

In this book of almost 800 pages, Jensen attempts to show that mental tests are not biased, but are objective instruments that assess individual differences. Seeking to dispel any doubts, he asserted, "Ability tests are explicitly designed to discriminate among individuals. I know of no ability tests that were ever designed for the purpose of discriminating *between* any social groups."[2]

Insisting that the average scoring differentials between groups are merely an "incidental by-product" of what the tests are designed to do, Jensen wrote, "Test discrimination between the statistical averages of different racial, cultural, or socioeconomic groups . . . is an incidental by-product of the test's discrimination among individuals *within* any group."[3]

In reality—which is precisely the opposite of what Jensen claims it to be—test discrimination among individuals *within* any group is the incidental by-product of tests constructed to discriminate *between* groups. Because the tests' class and racial bias ensures that some groups will be higher and others lower in the scoring hierarchy, the status of an individual member of a group is as a rule predetermined by the status of that group.

Comparisons and Construction

If we accept at face value Jensen's assurance that he knows of no tests designed to discriminate between groups, we must conclude that he is not only ill-informed about the nature of the tests, but also unaware that other testers have openly acknowledged what he so assiduously denies.

For example, in the 1930s—a time when the psychometricians and their supporters did not hesitate to acknowledge the connection between racial comparisons and test construction—three prominent social psychologists lauded the contribution of these comparisons to the "technique of testing." According to Gardner Murphy, Lois Barclay Murphy, and Theodore M. Newcomb,

> From a historical point of view, the dozens, nay hundreds of meticulous studies of race differences which have been provided are not to be belittled. They definitely contributed to the technique of testing, to the study of discrepancies obtained when groups are measured by various kinds of standard tests.[4]

The argument that studies of "race differences" should not be belittled because they contributed to the technique of testing seems a curious one, given that those who criticized the studies were most likely the same ones who criticized the tests. Nor are such studies a thing of the past. Although so obviously based on

the assumption of racial intelligence differentials as to be peculiarly vulnerable to criticism, they are still made today.[5] And
very often special tests are constructed to make them.

For example, many psychometricians admittedly construct
tests to compare the "cognitive processes" (another of the testers'
synonyms for "intelligence") of Third-World populations with
those of Western ones. Because these tests—all of them projections of the IQ method—consistently "find" Western populations superior, they give credibility to a myth that long preceded
the pseudoscience of mental measurement—that of "Western
mind, primitive mind."

According to this myth, Western populations have the ability
to abstract, while those in economically underdeveloped countries are restricted to concrete thinking. Since the myth was not
inspired by geography, it is hardly surprising that African-
Americans and other Western minorities are also assigned to the
primitive-mind category. And since those of lower socioeconomic status in general are also placed in the myth's lower
category, it might also be described as the myth of "upper-class
mind, lower-class mind."

The assumptions reflected in the myth—that different races,
nationalities, and classes have superior or inferior intelligence—
are built into the IQ method. Or, to put it another way, the IQ
method—as an analysis of its features shows—is a projection of
the myth.

II

The claim that mental tests are constructed to discriminate
among individuals according to their ability, not their race and
class, depends for its credibility on the testers' old standby,
mystification. To maintain an aura of credibility, the psychometricians need not mystify each variety of their tests. But they
must sustain the mystification of IQ tests, whose status affects
the credibility of testing as a whole.

The degree to which IQ tests have been mystified—or, to be

specific, that attention has been diverted from the fact that the tests take performance in class- and race-biased school systems as their measure of intelligence—can be gauged by the image the testers have created of the IQ, or intelligence quotient. After a person takes an IQ test, he or she is not described as having *made* a high, low, or average *score*, as would be the case if the test dealt with history, geography, or some other subject. Instead the individual is described as *having* a high, low, or average IQ. Obviously, if a person *has* an IQ, an IQ exists independently of IQ tests—which implies that IQ tests were brought into existence to measure an individual's intelligence quotient. But this image of the IQ quite literally reverses reality, since an IQ is an end product of the IQ method.

To calculate an IQ, the individual's "mental age" (which is determined by the relationship of the individual's score to the average score for that age group) is divided by her or his "chronological age," and the resulting quotient is multiplied by 100 to eliminate the decimal point. While this procedure seems simple enough, it is actually mystifying, since it involves the division of invention by reality. Further, reality is presented in a peculiar manner: "age," which *is* chronological, becomes "chronological age"—a redundancy occasioned by the testers' need to distinguish the actuality of age from the myth of mental age.

Taking issue with the psychologists and educators who use "IQ" and "intelligence" interchangeably, Robert L. Williams, a psychology professor and former president of the National Association of Black Psychologists, stated, "The intelligence quotient is a symbol which refers to a set of scores earned on a test, nothing more."[6]

"Normal Curve Is Their Banner"

One peculiarly mystifying aspect of IQ tests involves the bell-shaped curve formed by its scores. This scoring formation was inspired by a theory dating back to the eighteenth century, according to which the frequency distribution of real characteristics or phenomena forms a bell-shaped or "normal" curve. The theory was originally said to have universal applicability, but has long been known to apply only under certain circumstances.[7]

In any event, while certain phenomena do possess the characteristics for creating a normal curve, IQ tests do not; the testers *create the conditions* so the scores will form one, thus producing the illusion that the tests measure a "real" characteristic. At the same time, the testers can use the normal distribution—in which a group's place is made to correlate with its "normal" place in the social order—to uphold the claim that intelligence is distributed in different quantities in different groups.

"The normal curve is [the testers'] banner, but why should we believe that curve measures anything beyond scores that have been adjusted to fit loosely?" asked the physicist Philip Morrison.[8] Analyzing the process by which the bell-shaped distribution is achieved, he wrote: "[IQ] tests have been composed of items *selected* after trial for observed conformity with the normal distribution. Items that showed little correlation with the overall expectations, or with the results of previous tests of the kind, have been systematically excluded."[9]

"We Impose Our Will"

Perhaps more than any other feature of test construction, the "standardization sample" reveals how the test makers build their assumptions of class and racial intelligence differentials into IQ and other mental tests.

Starting with the original Stanford-Binet and for many years thereafter, tests were standardized on all-white groups, or samples. However, after protests against test bias in the sixties, the test makers began to include African-American and Latino children in some standardization samples. Although the testers have created the impression that a test so standardized is equitable for minorities, the fact is that the inclusion of minority-group members in a sample has no substantive effect on a test's outcome. The outcome is essentially determined by the nature of the test questions—as illustrated by the fact that tests whose samples included members of minorities yield the same relationship between race, socioeconomic status, and scores as that yielded by the first Stanford-Binet.

During the standardization process, candidate questions are administered to the sample. To be selected for the final test, a question must help establish the scoring norm for the group as a whole, as well as "subgroup" norms, which the test is supposed to replicate when released for general use. In other words, to be retained for the final test, an item must play its statistically predetermined role in creating a scoring distribution that places each subgroup in its predesignated place on the curve.

"We look at individual questions and see how many people get them right, and which people get them right," stated Andrew J. Strenio, Jr., author of *The Testing Trap* (1981), as he described the steps "we" would take if we wished to construct a test. "[We] consciously and deliberately select questions so that the kind of people who scored low on the pretest will score low on subsequent tests. We do the same for the middle and high scorers. We are imposing our will on the outcome."[10]

There is only one way the testers can impose their will on the outcome, that is, by selecting those items whose degree of bias for or against different "kind[s] of people" conforms to their prior assumption as to which kinds of people should be the higher, lower, or middle scorers.

III

Although he made no explicit reference to the controversy between the psychometricians and their critics over what IQ tests are constructed to do, Lawler accepted at face value the testers' version. The IQ test, he wrote, is "meant to discriminate children on the basis of general intelligence or intellectual capacity."[11]

Yet from Lawler's own remarks on the standardization sample one may get an entirely different impression of what IQ tests are meant to do. Discussing the original Stanford-Binet, he stated that Terman constructed it on "a large, representative sample of white, native-born Americans,"[12] that is, on native-born whites of varying socioeconomic levels. He went on to say: "A test based on the white, native-born population would necessarily be unrepresentative of populations not included in the sample."[13]

By maintaining that a sample is unrepresentative of a group whose members are excluded, Lawler accepted the premise that underlies either inclusion in or exclusion from a sample: that each population has its own level of intelligence.

When Terman excluded blacks and the foreign-born from his sample, he obviously acted on the assumption that they are inferior in intelligence. But when he included whites of different classes, he was not only acting on the premise that they are superior by virtue of race and nationality, but also, more subtly, on the assumption that they are relatively superior or inferior by virtue of class.

By the same token, when contemporary test makers include African-Americans in a sample, they are not providing equal-opportunity tests, but simply acting, albeit in a more sophisticated way, on the same assumption Terman made, namely, that blacks have a separate and unequal level of intelligence.

"National Intelligence"

"Terman's reasoning in selecting [his] sample seems to be that he wished to create a test of 'true American' intelligence, which would be the standard against which other peoples should be measured," stated Lawler, in what appears to be a criticism of Terman's objective.[14]

In reality, however, Lawler justified rather than rejected this objective. For example, discussing the relationship between the standardization sample and the distribution of scores, he wrote,

> Were the standardization sample overly representative of,
> say, urban, middle class children . . . [this] would result in a

non-normal distribution for the whole population which
would show the majority of the population as "below average in intelligence." This is of course not a sign of defectiveness of the national intelligence, but of the defectiveness of
the test.[15]

In one respect, Lawler's hypothetical test fulfills the test
makers' requirements. As one may easily infer, it has the standard class and racial bias, and so would rank the different groups
of test takers in the order established by a normal distribution.
But in another respect, the hypothetical test would create an
anomaly: the distribution it would produce, in which the majority scores below normal, would not only be a statistical absurdity
but would also conflict with the testers' notion of normality: it
would classify the majority, rather than the minority—African-
Americans, Puerto Ricans, Chicanos, Native Americans, and
others—as defective in intelligence.

By offering assurance that a nonnormal distribution is a sign
of test defectiveness, and not defectiveness of the "national
intelligence," Lawler assumed that a normal distribution reflects
the "distribution" of intelligence in the population. He also
made the corollary assumption that each nation has its own level
of intelligence—which is, of course, the rationale for such notions as "true American" intelligence and "Western mind, primitive mind."

IV

There are a great number of theses with which the IQ method
has a reciprocal relationship. The theses use IQ tests to support
their claims, while the tests are legitimated by the use the theses
make of them. It can, in fact, be difficult to make a clear
separation between the IQ method itself and some of these
theses.

Take, for example, the "deficit-model" concept. It can be seen
either as a concept inherent in IQ tests that has been elaborated
into a thesis, or as a thesis that uses IQ tests to uphold its

contentions. In any event, according to the deficit-model view, those groups whose scoring range is below the IQ test's statistical model of normal are deficient in the trait or traits allegedly measured by the tests. In other words, this view treats a statistical projection as representing the characteristics of real children. Williams observed:

> The deficit model assumes that black people are deficient when compared to whites in some measurable trait called intelligence, and that this deficiency is due to genetic or cultural factors or both. To support this notion, such terms as "heritability of IQ," "cultural deprivation," and "the disadvantaged" have been invented.[16]

Commenting on the social values intrinsic to the deficit model, he stated, "The deficit model assumes a set of acceptable, standard responses. If the black child gives a response that is not validated as acceptable by the norm, he is declared as deficient in his 'ability to comprehend and to size up certain social situations.' "[17]

Stressing the distinction that must be made between statistical models and real children, Williams stated, "Test inferiority is not to be equated with real inferiority."[18]

Making the Equation

A great many contemporary theses make the equation Williams warned against. All of the theses, whether advanced from an environmentalist or hereditarian standpoint, incorporate certain common assumptions. Herbert Ginsburg, a psychology professor and author of *The Myth of the Deprived Child* (1972), described these assumptions.

> [Poor] children are concrete in their thinking. They . . . lack the kind of abstraction which the "Western world" (and presumably not the non-Western) demands. The inability to think abstractly makes poor children incapable of satisfac-

tory work in school; their concrete mentality cannot cope
with the subtleties of academic subject matter.[19]

Hereditarians ascribe the alleged inability to abstract to genetic deficiencies in cognitive capacity in certain groups, while
environmentalists ascribe it to "stunted" cognition in the same
groups. In both cases, the ascription is justified by IQ and IQ-
type tests, that is, by using tests in which formal logical skills are
equated with the human ability to reason.

A peculiarly revealing example of this equation—which, again,
is based on the reductionist premise that reasoning ability
develops only in an academic context, rather than in the totality
of life experiences—was provided by Lawler: "Skill at solving
abstract problems [on IQ tests] . . . as well as the patience and
motivation needed to grapple with them, may very well correlate
with school success."[20]

Since school success is the IQ test's measure of intelligence, it
should come as no great surprise if skill at solving IQ-test
problems correlates with school success. But, having overlooked
this point, Lawler overlooked another, that is, the correlation
between school success and failure and superior and inferior
education along class and racial lines. Thus, according to Lawler,
school success is a matter of personal attributes found only in
those children who make higher IQ scores, while, conversely,
those who fail do so because they lack patience, motivation, and
the ability to abstract—in short, because they are the very model
of a deficit model.

According to the influential stunted-cognition thesis, children with lower IQ-test scores must overcome this alleged
condition before they can even begin to grasp academic subjects.[21] In a remark that suggests the identity of his position with
this thesis, as well as the relationship of both to the myth of
Western mind, primitive mind, Lawler stated,

[W]e are [not] denying the possibility of certain causal
connections between deficiencies or proficiencies in certain

primitive and fundamental concepts, and cognitive skills
and success or failure in school. In this sense remedial work
may have to go back to "basic" skills to recreate the foundations of cognitive development.[22]

By suggesting that children with lower IQ scores should "go
back to 'basic' skills," Lawler offered what can easily be construed as a rationale for the "back to basics" movement, which
attempts to restrict minority children in particular and children
of lower socioeconomic status in general to a minimal curriculum, or what many educators call the "Curriculum of Despair."[23]
Obviously, Lawler's remarks also justify the consignment of
children with lower IQ scores to EMR classes.

In contending that school failure may be explained by cognitive deficiencies that may be overcome by "recreat[ing] the
foundations of cognitive development," Lawler apparently intended to offer an optimistic prognosis. But if scholastic deficiencies may be explained by cognitive deficiencies, then efforts
to teach academic subjects may be expected to fail. Such is the
outlook inherent in any thesis that places the onus for school
performance on the children rather than the schools and the
society.

V

In 1963, a young man with little teaching experience was assigned to a class of thirty-six sixth-graders in Harlem. The
school system had already made it clear to the teacher, Herbert
Kohl, that the children were expected to fail. Kohl had also read
many articles that claimed children such as these are "emotionally and culturally deprived, had learning difficulties, and
might in fact be genetically inferior."[24]

On the first day of school, Kohl was given the children's
cumulative records, including their IQ scores. He locked the
records away ("The children would tell me who they were").[25]
He found there was no complete set of arithmetic books ("It was
as though, encouraged to believe that the children couldn't do

arithmetic . . . the administration decided not to waste money on arithmetic books").[26] The readers were boring and unreal ("the world of Dick and Jane").[27] For the next six weeks, Kohl tried to teach the official curriculum; he found it "hopeless."[28]

Kohl began taking his cues from the children. He picked up on one of their slang expressions: "psyches." He told them it came from a Greek word. Tracing the word to its source led the class to Greek mythology. And it led Kohl to the African and Asian sources of the myths, and from there to research on early African and Asian societies ("As this whole new world opened for me I shared it with the children").[29] The class also traced the origins of names; one child said that his brother called himself John X because "X meant unknown and his original African name was unknown."[30]

Kohl brought books into the class, ranging from works on Greek architecture and art to Langston Hughes and J.D. Salinger ("Some children hardly read at all, others devoured whatever was in the room. The same is true of my friends").[31]

The class became "word-hungry and concept-hungry":

> Mr. Kohl, what do you call it when a person repeats the same thing over and over and can't stop?
>
> What do you call a person who brags and thinks he's big but is really weak inside?
>
> Mr. Kohl, is there a word that says that something has more than one meaning?[32]

The children moved from vocabulary to writing, discovering the need for it "just as the Mesopotamians and Egyptians did."[33] Having discovered writing, they produced remarkable books, stories, poems.

The children's study of Greek mythology also stimulated them in other ways. One child, a talented artist, made a scale model of the Parthenon. Two other children built a clay model of a volcano, then asked for a chemistry book that would show them how to simulate an eruption. They got the book, but there was difficulty in getting scientific equipment for the class. The children led Kohl to a hall cabinet where years of science supplies—enough for the whole school—had been locked away. And the children knew why: because they were students in a Harlem school.

That Kohl found it impossible to teach the standard curriculum stood the children in good stead in terms of a real education. But it did not help a bit when it came to a harsh reality of the school system—the compulsory IQ and achievement tests the children faced halfway through the year. Kohl tried to coach them, just as white, middle-class children are coached for tests. But there was little time left—not to mention that the children had spontaneously rejected the IQ method. "I frequently found that some of the children were deliberately choosing wrong answers because they had clever explanations for their choices. They had to be convinced that the people who created objective tests believed as an article of faith that all the questions they made up had one and only one correct answer."[34]

The children were "almost ready" for their reading tests, and this was reflected in their scores. (That they had read widely does not mean they had acquired the "reading skills" needed for these tests; presumably Kohl coached them in those skills.)

The children who had performed so remarkably in class did not, however, fare well on the IQ tests; the outcome was "close to a disaster." The children tried to put the testing experience in perspective. "[The children] knew that the test preparation was not all there was to education, that the substance of their work, the novels and stories, the poems and projects they created, were the essential thing no matter how the external world chose to judge them."[35]

But the external world was still what the children had to face; their teacher had offered them an alternative class, but no one would offer them an alternative world. As one of the thirty-six children told him some time after she had left his class for others, "Mr. Kohl, one good year isn't enough."[36]

The Symbiotic Connection

I

Science develops. Pseudoscience is static. The distinction is elementary. So elementary it seems inconceivable that, in the late twentieth century, the hereditarian-environmentalist debate could be portrayed as scientific, when it is just where it was when it started in the late eighteenth century.

In a description of the debate in its early phase that could serve equally well as a report on its current status, the historian George M. Fredrickson wrote: "The great unresolved question was whether *alleged* differences in intelligence . . . between Caucasians and various non-European 'races' were attributable to their having lived in different environments or reflected the fact that they belonged to what amounted to different species" (emphasis added).[1]

The nature-nurture debate—which takes an *allegation* of racial intelligence differentials as a given and argues over the cause of the assumed differentials—got under way in this country under the aegis of Thomas Jefferson. "More than any other single person he framed the terms of the debate still carried on today," stated the historian Winthrop D. Jordan.[2] It was in his *Notes on*

85

Virginia (1784) that the immensely complex Jefferson—he was both author of the Declaration of Independence and a slave-holder—outlined the terms on which an ongoing, informal argument could be converted into a relatively formal debate. Taking as his premise the assumption of black mental inferiority, he wrote: "Comparing [blacks] by their faculties of memory, reason, and imagination, it appears to me that in memory they are equal to the whites; in reason much inferior, as I think one could scarcely be found capable of tracing and comprehending the investigations of Euclid."[3]

While environmentalists of the day argued that the conditions of slavery had produced an inferior mentality in blacks, Jefferson attributed the alleged inferiority to biology: "it is not their condition . . . but nature, which has produced the distinction."[4]

Had Jefferson concluded with this categorical assertion of "natural" black inferiority, he would have done nothing to stimulate the support he sought from science. Therefore he proceeded to recast his flatly hereditarian assertion into an "opinion . . . [that] must be hazarded with great diffidence." He then wrote:

> To justify a general conclusion requires many observations, even where the subject may be submitted to the Anatomical knife, to Optical glasses, to analysis by fire, or by solvents. How much more then where it is a faculty, not a substance, we are examining; where it eludes the research of all the senses; . . . where the effects of those which are present or absent bid defiance to calculation.[5]

Jefferson seemed to offer a model for scientific investigation. Actually, however, he urged that scientific considerations be ignored; he acknowledged that mental "faculties" are not a substance and so elude research, yet he proposed observations designed to justify the prior assumption of racial differences in these conceptualized traits. He also admitted that the effects of the so-called faculties "bid defiance to calculation," yet he pressed science to take a pseudoscientific path—one that would lead to an effort to calculate the incalculable, i.e., to quantify the presumed effects of hypothesized traits.

"Last Stand"

Some of those who took issue with Jefferson's position rejected the claim of black mental inferiority. But most who differed did so from the standpoint of environmentalism, which was influential among antislavery forces. Although the point is generally overlooked, environmentalism also had adherents among the "colonizationalists," who opposed abolition.[6]

By the early nineteenth century, biological determinism was entering a long period of ascendancy. The hereditarians had an advantage during this time because craniometrics (unlike psychometrics) could not be used to advantage by environmentalists. The hereditarian interpretation of the alleged racial and class intelligence differentials prevailed until the 1930s. At that point, environmentalism—greatly assisted by the growing worldwide revulsion against the Nazis' claim of biologically superior and inferior races—began to enter its period of ascendancy.

With the defeat of the Nazis, environmentalism continued to gain adherents. By the 1950s, it had become so influential that the belief arose in some circles that hereditarianism was being driven into permanent retirement. Of course, these circles could hardly deny that hereditarians were still at work, but they could classify the latter's activities as merely "rear-guard." Then in the 1960s, there came what some interpreted as definitive evidence of the rout of hereditarianism: the government launched nationwide education programs based on environmentalist concepts. Yet just when the triumph of environmentalism seemed assured, the *Harvard Educational Review* published Jensen's article.

But even at this point, many environmentalists—basing their positions on the widespread opposition to Jensen's claims, while apparently ignoring his support from powerful quarters—believed that hereditarianism was making its "last stand." As it turned out, the only correlation between this prophecy and its fulfillment was a negative one; in the same period when this soothing prediction was made, yet another biological-determinist thesis, "sociobiology," was ushered in.

II

Since biological determinism is an ideological thesis, it is well suited to revivals. Its supporters simply disregard scientific disproof and bring back their multipurpose rationale for the social status quo in yet another form.

The latest version of the thesis arrived at center stage in 1975 when Harvard University Press published *Sociobiology: The New Synthesis*, by E.O. Wilson, a Harvard zoologist. Since then sociobiology, which holds that the social behavior of human beings is to all intents and purposes genetically coded, has been hailed by powerful academic circles and the media as a "new discipline."

In a quite obvious effort to distinguish their thesis from Jensen's, and so forestall the attacks his encountered, the sociobiologists initially avoided emphasizing race. Instead they focused on gender. They advanced an inclusive genetic justification for women's inferior social status, which was soon followed by various subtheses, one of them on women and mathematics. This subthesis—which ignores the obstacles placed between females and those studies traditionally treated as a male prerogative, as well as the math tests on which women's performance equals men's—revives the kind of claims once made by the craniometricians. It attributes the gender scoring differentials on SAT math subtests to a supposed gender differential in brain structure.[7]

Heritability Claim Revived

In maintaining that the inferior social status of women is genetically determined, sociobiology also offered, by implication, a rationale for superior and inferior status along class and racial lines. The rationale became explicit when the sociobiologists linked racist attitudes to genetic causes, maintaining, as one put it, that such attitudes are "more or less built into the species."[8] That the "new discipline" is simply a variant of earlier hereditarian positions became particularly evident when Wilson reiterated Jensen's heritability claim: "It has clearly been established that intelligence is, for the most part, inherited."[9]

But nothing of the kind has been established; every effort to uphold hereditarian claims—from Galton's to Jensen's—has been proven false. For instance, to support his claim that intelligence—i.e., an IQ score—is 80 percent heritable, Jensen used correlations from studies of the IQ scores of twins. The psychologist Leon Kamin exposed the studies as total falsifications.[10] Moreover, the practice of estimating the heritability of IQ scores has been proved false. "IQ scores and correlations . . . based on them have as much scientific validity as horoscopes," concluded the astrophysicist David A. Layzer.[11]

Jensen also alleged that there are "intelligence genes," and that they are present in larger numbers in whites than in blacks. Wilson, too, invoked intelligence genes to support the claim of a genetic basis for the social order. Chorover wrote: "Despite Professor Wilson's assertions to the contrary, there is not an iota of evidence to suggest that there are genes . . . for intelligence. . . . The genes in question are genes of a mythical kind which have been invented to buttress certain social preconceptions."[12]

As sociobiology became entrenched as a "new discipline," it began to enjoy greater protection from public scrutiny. Thus it has become an increasingly potent means for reinforcing the preconception of the social order as a reflection of a natural order.

III

Many environmentalists have condemned hereditarianism as "scientific" racism and a rationale for the social status quo. Valuable as these critiques are, they are also an anomaly, since the environmentalists' own thesis is part of the process that keeps biological determinism alive, that is, as a thesis that accepts the claimed racial and class intelligence differentials and advances its own interpretation of the disparities it assumes, environmentalism necessarily sustains the rival hereditarian interpretation of the presupposed differentials.

Since the environmentalists' interpretation of the claimed intelligence differences reinforces the claim itself, one may wonder why there has been so little criticism of it. One reason is that critiques by environmentalists of hereditarianism's social role have legitimated the environmentalist thesis. Another is that the hereditarians' right-wing diatribes against environmentalism have helped shield it from valid criticism, while enhancing the benign, nonracist image it has acquired.

Environmentalism's egalitarian image makes it very useful to the testing establishment. This point is made evident by the following statement from the Committee on Ability Testing: "Given the assumptions that underlay the [hereditarian] view, testing programs could easily serve to preserve the existing social order."[13]

While sounding quite radical, this statement actually suggests that testing programs serve as a rationale for the social order only when interpreted from a hereditarian standpoint. That environmentalism also serves as a rationale for the social order can, however, be determined by examining the work of environmentalists—and not only that of conservative environmentalists, but also the work of environmentalists who wanted to make changes in the status quo. As a particularly significant example of the latter point, let us look at Otto Klineberg's work.

Klineberg's Study

To answer the hereditarians' claim of "selective migration"—i.e., that there was a North-South scoring differential for blacks on the army IQ tests because the blacks who came North were genetically superior—Klineberg undertook a large-scale study, whose results were published in 1935 (*Negro Intelligence and Selective Migration*).

In this study, which became highly influential, Klineberg set out to show that there was no intelligence differential between blacks who migrated and those who stayed in the South. To this end, he compared the school records of African-American children who left southern cities with the records of those who stayed. His preference was to use IQ tests for this purpose, but few of the children had been tested. In any event, he considered his procedure acceptable because "intelligence tests . . . have almost always been standardized against school records."[14]

Klineberg's study also included an experiment in which IQ tests were given to southern-born blacks attending Harlem schools. When the scores showed an increase roughly related to the children's length of residence in New York, he concluded that the "present superiority of the northern over the southern Negro may be explained by the more favorable environment, rather than by selective migration."[15] Specifically, Klineberg was saying that northern blacks were superior in intelligence to southern blacks by virtue of superior schooling (albeit schooling inferior to that of northern whites). He also concluded that it might be possible to bring the intelligence of blacks "up to the white level."[16]

Klineberg conducted his study with the exemplary aim of rebutting the selective-migration thesis, but the study itself reinforced from an environmentalist standpoint the hereditarians' claims that whites are superior in intelligence to blacks and that IQ tests and school performance are measures of intelligence.

Klineberg also provided a peculiarly striking example of the symbiosis between hereditarianism and environmentalism when he decided to "measure" the intelligence of the adults, i.e., those who made the decision to stay in or leave the South, by the school records of the children. To justify this proxy arrangement, he asserted that there is "probably a certain amount of mental similarity between members of the same family." The extent of the similarity, he added, was an "open question."[17] So, in attempting to reduce the significance of his concession to hereditarianism, he took a position that could only encourage a debate over race, intelligence, and heritability percentages.

Finally, Klineberg's speculation that it might be possible to bring the blacks' "inferior" level of intelligence up to the "superior" level of the whites was a prelude to the treatment this false issue would be accorded three decades later, when "compensatory education" was introduced—and with it, a controversy that would have grave consequences for public education.

IV

"Compensatory education has been tried and it apparently has failed," asserted Jensen in the opening line of his notorious "How Much Can We Boost IQ and Scholastic Achievement?"[18]

Since the article was published in the *Harvard Educational Review*, it was of course unavailable to the general public. If it had been available, most people would have found the phrase "compensatory education" unfamiliar. But in reading on, they would have learned that Jensen was speaking in particular of a well-known project, Operation Head Start. The project had been launched with great fanfare by the Johnson administration in 1965, a time of nationwide calls for civil rights and an end to poverty. These comprehensive demands were accompanied by a special and insistent call for "quality, integrated education."

In some respects, Head Start was an accommodation to this demand, and in others a barrier against fulfilling it. On the one hand, the new project represented a historic advance. It provided children of lower socioeconomic status with their first opportunity for preschooling, and it also offered them such benefits as free meals and free medical and dental care. On the other hand, the assumption underlying Head Start, as a compensatory-education program, was that children, particularly the African-American children, had to be compensated for deficient intelligence. Consistent with this orientation, Head Start's assigned objective was to "boost" IQ scores.

The administration designated Head Start as one of the first parts of its "war on poverty." The reasoning behind this was described by a writer for *Psychology Today:* "The founders of the Great Society hoped that the children of the poor would become as intelligent . . . as the children of the middle class, and thus break the cycle of poverty."[19]

So, at a time when the administration was presumably committed to a war on poverty, it was sending out the message that the onus for poverty does not lie on the society but on the poor themselves. But instead of offering a bluntly hereditarian rationale for the social order—i.e., asserting it is impossible for poor people to break out of poverty because of a genetic deficiency in intelligence—it offered a more subtle, environmentalist one: poor children might break out of poverty if they responded to efforts to boost their intelligence.

In the same period that the administration assumed this philosophical stance on breaking out of poverty, it also commissioned two reports that would help undermine the educational and social programs it had so recently inaugurated.

Two Reports

Because of the sensationalized treatment it got from the media, Jensen's thesis seemed to arrive like the proverbial bolt from the blue. But in reality, two environmentalist documents had helped to prepare a receptive climate for it. These documents—which also provoked intense opposition—were the Moynihan and Coleman reports.

The Coleman Report was published by the Department of Health, Education, and Welfare in 1966.[20] Its author, the sociologist James S. Coleman, suggested that there really is no need to eliminate racial and class differentials in the quality of education because, he held, the quality of schooling has little effect on academic performance. In Coleman's view, school performance is determined by family environment, which produces intelligence/ability levels that correspond to the family's class status and race. To support his claims, he used the class and racial scoring differentials from standardized tests.

One year earlier, the Department of Labor had published the Moynihan Report.[21] Its author, Daniel P. Moynihan, then Assistant Secretary of Labor, held that a heritage of social inequality — specifically, a history of slavery, discrimination, and poverty — had made blacks inferior to whites. To support this claim, he cited the results of ability/intelligence tests.

The Moynihan Report was a classic expression of the "social pathology" position, which appears to place the onus for the alleged inferiority of African-Americans on the social order, and in so doing to assume an aura of social concern. While the central feature of this thesis is its falsification of the effects of racism and poverty on their victims, it also has other aspects worth noting: it attributes the claimed inferiority of blacks to the social evils of the *past*, while suggesting that the *present* society offers blacks opportunities they cannot take advantage of because of deficient intelligence. (The thesis was later adapted so that it could also be applied to whites of lower socioeconomic status.)

By thus placing responsibility for their social inequality on blacks themselves, Moynihan — later the author of the doctrine of "benign neglect" — attempted to remove the question of black social inequality from the arena of social action. (One of President Johnson's most publicized speeches was based on the Moynihan Report.)

At the same time that the Coleman and Moynihan reports were being widely promoted, certain groups (including ETS) were monitoring Head Start. By 1966, studies began to appear that generated doubts as to whether Head Start was carrying out its assignment to boost IQ scores.[22] Thus a controversy over Head Start was in the making during the Johnson administration; it escalated when Jensen's article was published early in the

Nixon era. "The Jensen report was . . . well known to the Nixon Administration when the budgets for compensatory education were being sharply reduced," observed Robert Williams.[23]

One of the first to hail Jensen's thesis was Moynihan. He was not the only one to switch from a social-pathology to a hereditarian position. In fact, until just before he revived hereditarianism, Jensen himself was an adherent of the social-pathology thesis. That both men made this switch is far less surprising than it may have seemed; both retained their primary assumption of racial and class intelligence differentials and changed only their secondary one, i.e., they switched from the family environment to the family genes as the carrier of the alleged mental inferiority.

The Debating Circle

In the years since Jensen's article appeared, the controversy around Head Start has almost always been portrayed as one between those who defend the environmentalist compensatory-education concept and those who assail it from a hereditarian standpoint. Almost always missing from the picture are the views of those who believe the nation's first public preschool program—whose availability is still nowhere near what it should be—was saddled with a concept and objective that left it vulnerable to attack. One of those who criticized the program with the aim of changing its orientation was Williams, who stated, "If the goal and objective of Head Start . . . and other compensatory education programs is that of 'boosting IQ,' then the goal is misput, inappropriate and irrelevant."[24]

The format for the Head Start debate was established by the *Harvard Educational Review*, which followed Jensen's article with articles by an invited group of environmentalists and hereditarians. Soon the debating circle expanded greatly; the two basic positions (albeit in many variant forms) were reiterated in other periodicals, as well as in many books.

Although the debate's ostensible subject was whether Head Start had failed, its real subject was the assumed failure of the children, that is, whether they were born failures because of a genetic deficiency in intelligence, or whether they had failed because the program had not done enough to compensate for the postnatal circumstances that allegedly left them with deficient intelligence.

Among the debaters who took the latter position was J. McVicker Hunt, a psychologist whose ideas were a prime influence on Head Start. In a book published in 1961, he helped codify the variant of environmentalism that prevailed at the time and remains highly influential today, namely, early-childhood determinism.[25] Although the belief that the child's environment during his or her first years determines the adult's characteristics is an old one, Hunt's and other modern versions focus on one characteristic, "intelligence."

For this view to accept a child as normal in intelligence, the child's experiences must match those that are called for by the norms of mental measurement. If the child's experiences diverge from those called for by these arbitrary, biased norms, she or he is classified deficient in intelligence. To explain the alleged deficiency, early-childhood determinism subsumes two related theses, social pathology and "cultural deprivation."

According to the latter concept, children who come from "deviant" families, or families that are not white and middle class, suffer from cultural/verbal deprivation, which stunts their intelligence and produces a "verbal deficit." (Jensen was associated with this position when he was a social pathologist; later he decided the alleged verbal deficit is due to genetic rather than cultural deprivation.)[26]

The verbal-deprivation thesis was inspired in particular by the British sociologist Basil Bernstein, who claimed that the speech of British working-class children is underdeveloped. American psychologists elaborated on his thesis for application, in particular, to speakers of Black English.

"[T]he language of culturally deprived children . . . is not merely an underdeveloped version of standard English, but is a basically nonlogical mode of expressive behavior," according to two specialists in compensatory education.[27] To support this claim, the early-childhood determinists used IQ and IQ-type tests. They also conducted a host of laboratory experiments to support a corollary claim that the mothers of "verbally deprived" children are especially responsible for depriving their children of the stimulation they need for normal development. (Ironically, this concept—which assumes a woman's place is in the home—was advanced at a time when women were moving into the work force in greater numbers than ever.)

The experiments were conducted in a way sure to alienate the subjects. "[M]ost childhood development literature relies overwhelmingly on laboratory situations such as . . . a mother and child observed by a researcher who is a stranger," noted de Lone.[28] It is evident that under such conditions verbal interaction between mothers and children in general would be significantly reduced. But this would apply in particular to African-Americans, who historically have used noncommunicativeness as a defense in hostile situations.

Occasionally the early-childhood determinists step out of their laboratories and into their subjects' homes. But the change of locale is essentially irrelevant; wherever they go, they filter their observations through their preconceptions. As Joseph White, a professor of psychology and psychiatry, observed:

> [The white psychologist] enters the observational net of the black home . . . with a deficit or weakness hypothesis, so that his recommended programs are based upon some concept of enrichment defined by the dominant culture— from Head Start to Upward Bound, to language enrichment programs, etc. Somehow the analysis is always corrective; implied is always some deficit that the child brings to the situation from his home. This analysis had pre-psychological origins, and it is a clear carryover from slavery . . . that there is something inferior about the black child, and, therefore, the black man.[29]

The verbal-deficit view of black children prevails among educational psychologists despite the fact that linguists have produced irrefutable evidence of its falsity.

Inverted Logic

"Operation Head Start is designed to repair the child, rather than the school; to the extent that it is based upon this inverted logic, it is bound to fail," declared the sociolinguist William Labov in 1972, as he expressed his opposition to Head Start's adoption of the verbal-deficit thesis.[30] Labov, one of the linguists who have made scientific studies of Black English,[31] also stated, "That educational psychology should be strongly influenced by a theory so false to the facts of language is unfortunate; but that children should be the victims of this ignorance is intolerable."[32]

Labov did not use IQ or IQ-type tests in his study, nor did he conduct conventional experiments. Instead he devised methods of communicating with black children that elicited their real way of speaking. The results of this study—which show that Black English is systematic and rule-governed in its grammar, phonology, and semantics—shattered the myth of these children as speakers of an underdeveloped, nonlogical language.

> The concept of verbal deprivation has no basis in social reality. In fact, black children in the urban ghettos receive a great deal of verbal stimulation . . . and participate fully in a highly verbal culture. They have the same basic vocabulary, possess the same capacity for conceptual learning, and use the same logic as anyone else who learns to speak and understand English.[33]

Labov also said that "if there is a failure of logic involved here, it is surely in the approach of the verbal deprivation theorists, rather than in the mental abilities of the children concerned."[34]

Revising the Thesis

Soon after the results of Labov's study were first published (in the late sixties), a number of psychologists offered counterarguments. Hunt, for instance, made slight revisions in the original deprivation thesis.[35] Others took a more complex approach. For example, Michael Cole and Jerome Bruner asserted that Labov's criticism of the deficit thesis should be accepted. But at the same time, they advanced a replacement for it: a "differences" concept. As these two cross-cultural psychologists put it, the "educational difficulties" of minority children should be seen in terms of a *"difference"* rather than as a "special kind of intellectual disease."[36]

According to the Cole-Bruner thesis, individuals from minority cultures may not function well in the dominant culture because they have not transferred skills they already possess to the other cultural context. Yet the real question is not simply one of *transferring* skills, but of learning new ones as well. In this respect, Cole and Bruner were not hopeful; i.e., they suggested that members of certain groups may have cognitive problems that prevent them from acquiring the skills they lack. For instance, discussing what they called "cultural amplifiers," they reasserted the old claim of a correlation between higher education and higher intelligence in a particularly mystifying way:

> An example of a middle-class cultural amplifer that operates to increase the thought processes of those who employ it is the discipline loosely referred to as "mathematics." . . . If one does not cultivate mathematical skills, the result is "functional incompetence," an inability to use this kind of technology. Whether or not compensatory techniques can then correct "functional incompetence" is an important, but unexplored, question.[37]

So, according to this thesis, if one does not cultivate mathematical skills—or, to put it accurately, if one is of minority or lower socioeconomic status and does not have an equal opportunity to cultivate them—one will not only suffer from "functional incompetence" in mathematics, but may not be able to learn it at all. (This view also has important implications for the alleged relationship between gender and the ability to acquire math skills.) Thus, while Cole and Bruner criticized the cultural-deficit thesis, their own thesis also ascribed the scholastic problems faced by African-American children to an *internal* barrier rather than to institutional racism and inferior education.

In a book published the same year as his article with Bruner (1971), Cole also asserted his agreement with Labov, but again took a position that pointed in the opposite direction: "[W]e find ourselves very much in agreement with Labov and others who criticize the psychologist's and educator's view of cultural deprivation. However, we are also concerned with the fact that, for whatever cause, minority-group performance in a wide variety of educational settings is such as to insure their continued low position in American society."[38]

Cole presented us with a dilemma. As he put it, minorities cannot hope to move from a lower to a higher status unless their uniformly poor scholastic performance changes; at the same time, his remarks suggest that there is not much incentive for society to make changes in their educational settings, i.e., whatever the setting, their performance stays the same.

Although Cole held that scholastic performance of African-Americans and other minorities is uniformly poor in a variety of settings, a look at the settings shows little variation: they are quite uniformly characterized by testing, tracking, segregation, racism, and (as Cole acknowledged) the assumption of cultural deprivation. A further look shows that in those exceptional situations where elements in the settings are changed—including the assumption of cognitive inequality—the performance of minority students also changes.

Finally, while the cultural-deprivation thesis and its variants are dominant, many educators and psychologists dissent. Instead of searching for something in the children that renders them unable to perform in an academic setting and also assures them a low status in the social order, they locate the cause of poor scholastic performance and low social status in the schools and the society.

The Barrier

Despite the continuing dominance of the claims of black cognitive inferiority, the linguistic evidence of black cognitive equality has had significant repercussions. There was, for example, the ruling in 1979 by Judge Charles Joiner, Jr., in *Martin Luther King, Jr., Elementary School et al. v. Ann Arbor School District Board*, which the media dubbed the "Black English" case.

Although the media created the impression that Judge Joiner ordered that black children be taught in Black English, he actually handed down an entirely different decision. He held that the school board's failure to teach the children to read in the "standard English" of the sciences, professions, and commerce was a denial of equal opportunity. Explicitly rejecting the claim that an internal barrier prevents these children from learning, he found,

> If a barrier exists because of the language used by the children . . . , it exists not because the teachers and students cannot understand each other, but because in the process of attempting to teach the children how to speak standard English the students are made somehow to feel inferior and are thereby turned off from the learning process.[39]

The trial also had another significant feature: the defendants did not produce a single psychologist, educator, linguist, or other witness to testify that speakers of Black English are "verbally impoverished," "nonlogical," or have any of the other cognitive deficiencies the cultural/verbal deprivationists have claimed they possess.[40]

V

The eighteenth-century environmentalist argument that the conditions of slavery produced an inferior mentality in blacks was revived, with minimal updating, when Moynihan claimed that a heritage of slavery and discrimination had produced an inferior mentality in blacks. His approach has become increasingly influential.

Among the writers on IQ tests who follow this approach—i.e., who accept the tests as a measure of intelligence and offer the social-pathology interpretation of the racial scoring differentials—was Gould, who spoke of a "link" between blacks' IQ scores and the "history of slavery and racism."[41]

Lawler also advanced the social-pathology argument when, for example, he chastised Jensen for not considering the "slave exploitation" and "four hundred year history of racism" in explaining "Black-white IQ differences."[42] Lawler's approach was, however, unusual: he not only put forth this argument in its classic form, but also superimposed Marxist terminology on it. He ascribed the alleged class and racial intelligence differentials to the "division of labor."

Expounding his division-of-labor thesis, he asserted that "biological differences" among children have "greater impact" when the children are younger or, as he put it, when their activities are "relatively primitive." He continued:

> We have argued that the truly social forms of development of intelligence are based on the historical division of labor in class society. While such class-based forces would be active from the very beginning of the child's life, their effect would become all the more pronounced as the child reaches the more complex, developed states of intelligence. At this point social-class relations including racial discrimination begin to dominate in determining the relative standing of the children in given age groups in the population.[43]

Contrary to this schematic interpretation—in which social phenomena become increasingly important as biological ones become less and less so—the process of human development involves a dynamic relationship between biological and social factors. It is also a process in which the individual plays an active role. As a result, the process does not *become* "truly social" at some advanced point in the child's life, but is so from the start.

Because he interpreted human development from a reductionist, cultural-determinist standpoint, Lawler saw the child as
playing a passive rather than an increasingly active role in her or
his own development. This led him to misinterpret the effects of
racism and class discrimination on the child, that is, to see these
negative social factors as phenomena that stunt the cognitive
development of their objects. This is why he concluded that
when children reach the "more complex, developed states of
intelligence" — or, to be precise, when the children have taken IQ
tests and been ranked accordingly — they form a hierarchy in
which intelligence correlates with class and race.

Lawler defined his division-of-labor and development-of-in-
telligence thesis as a "Marxist" form of environmentalism. This
is ironic, considering that it provides a rationale for a social order
to which Marx's antagonism is axiomatic.

"Educator Needs Educating"

An added irony attaches itself to Lawler's definition of his thesis
as Marxist when one discovers that Marx himself explicitly
rejected the tenets of environmentalism.

> The materialist doctrine that men are products of circum-
> stances and upbringing, and that, therefore, changed men
> are products of other circumstances and changed upbring-
> ing, forgets that it is men that change circumstances and
> that the educator himself needs educating.[44]

The view that human beings are agents in their own development is supported by modern research. As Ginsburg pointed
out,

> The evidence shows that . . . from the day of birth (and even
> before), the infant is active . . . . The infant quickly learns to
> distinguish among various features of the immediate envi-
> ronment and to modify his behavior in accord with its
> demands. Yet the environment does not simply shape and

mould his behavior . . . . Instead the infant plays an active
role in determining the course of his own development. To a
significant degree, he controls the process of learning and
interprets the data of experience.[45]

Nor is such activity limited to children from relatively affluent
backgrounds.

By virtue of their humanity, poor children are active organ-
isms. Like everyone else, they organize their own learning,
they are curious about the world, they practice what needs
to be learned . . . . Poor children take an active role in
devising solutions to the reality that confronts them.[46]

The active, purposeful response of an individual faced with
problems is also characteristic of human beings faced as a group
with problems. The sociologist Joyce A. Ladner—in remarks that
challenge environmentalism in general and its social-pathology
variant in particular—observed:

Many books have been written about the Black community.
. . . By and large, they have attempted to analyze and
describe the pathology which allegedly characterizes the
lives of its inhabitants while at the same time making its
residents responsible for its creation . . . .

Few authorities on the Black community have written about
the vast amount of strength and adaptability of the people.
They have ignored the fact that this community is a force
that not only acts upon its residents but which is also acted
upon. Black people are involved in a dynamic relationship
with their . . . environment in that they both influence and
are influenced by it.[47]

VI

Jefferson's assertion that "one could scarcely find" a black person
"capable of tracing and comprehending" Euclid soon proved
embarrassing. Most blacks were slaves, and as such barred from

learning to read, let alone being permitted to study mathematics. Yet it was a black mathematician and astronomer who confronted Jefferson with the most telling repudiation of his views.

Benjamin Banneker, a free black from Maryland, was one of this country's pioneer scientists. His contributions included the establishment by astronomical observation of the latitude and longitude lines for what would become Washington, D.C.[48] He also produced an almanac, a significant achievement for that time.

The almanac, which was widely used, included an unusual feature, a statement from the men who printed it. The views of these Baltimore printers contrast strikingly with those of environmentalists. While the latter hold that the prejudice confronting blacks stunts their mental development, the printers stressed that prejudice distorts the mental perceptions of those influenced by it. Banneker's almanac, they declared, demonstrated that "mental Powers and Endowments are not the exclusive Excellence of white People, but that the Rays of Science may alike illumine the Minds of Men of every Clime . . . particularly those whom Tyrant-Custom hath too long taught us to depreciate as a Race inferior in intellectual Capacity."[49]

In an (unsuccessful) effort to enlist Jefferson in the antislavery cause, Banneker sent him a copy of the almanac. He accompanied it with a letter in which he made a scathing contrast between Jefferson's attitude to the "tyranny of the British crown" and his own tyranny as a slaveholder. In a pointed rebuke to Jefferson's claims that blacks are incapable of understanding Euclid, Banneker observed that "we are a race of beings" who have long been regarded as "scarcely capable of mental endowments." But, he assured Jefferson, blacks are endowed with "the same faculties" as whites. Finally—in a remark that offers the clue to the fallacy of environmentalism—he spoke of the "many difficulties and disadvantages which I have had to encounter."[50]

Because environmentalists see human beings as products of circumstances, they believe that mental development can take place only under favorable conditions. Failing to recognize that individuals are active agents in their own development, they do not see that the human ability to reason, to think logically, develops not only under advantageous conditions but also as individuals strive to cope with and overcome disadvantageous ones.

The Testers, South Africa, and the Third World

I

Unbeknown to this country's millions of test takers or, as the case may be, their parents, a special connection exists between mental testing in this country and in Africa. This connection arises from the testing expeditions conducted by U.S. psychometricians in Africa since the days of colonialism.

In reading about these expeditions, one discovers that certain concepts, which are treated as innovations by the testers, actually had their origins in notions advanced years ago by anthropologists. One also learns that the classic rationale for testing in this country—a professed interest in individual differences, accompanied by assurances that comparisons between groups are merely incidental by-products of comparisons among individuals—is not exported. When testing in Third-World countries, the psychometricians openly acknowledge their abiding interest in group, or cross-cultural comparisons.

The interest, however, is not reciprocated. After many colonized countries attained their independence, they began to close their doors to Western researchers. In 1973, the president of the International Association for Cross-Cultural Psychology, Gustav Jahoda, noted,

> [T]here are signs that the doors of developing countries may be closing to psychologists. It is becoming more difficult for researchers from outside to get permission to carry out projects, and the chances are that this trend will continue. . . . [T]he invasion by foreign researchers is apt to be viewed as a more or less subtle form of exploitation.[1]

Jahoda was not suggesting that Western researchers resign themselves to exclusion, but rather warning that they must counter the sentiment leading to it. The impossibility of their doing so is evident from his description of the nature of cross-cultural studies: "Traditionally the cross-cultural study is one in which Western industrial cultures are compared with pre-literate tribal ones."[2]

By using the term "pre-literate," one ignores the fact that certain populations have not had the opportunity to become literate and suggests instead that their intelligence or cognitive processes have not arrived, whether for cultural/environmental or biological reasons, at the level required for literacy.

Early Times

If the sociopolitical character of cross-cultural comparisons is quite evident from the foregoing quotations, it is often made even more explicit. For example, at the time when many African nations had recently attained political independence, an American professor of psychology, Arthur G.J. Cryns, wrote:

> The process of Africa's de-colonization . . . makes the question of African intelligence one of utmost actuality and significance. The rapid strides which the continent has to

make in its transition from . . . under-development towards better ways of life, and the urgent need for indigenous leadership . . . constitute problems which directly refer to the question, whether the autochthonous African has the potentialities to deal effectively with such problems.[3]

Thus Cryns offered a paradoxical interpretation: the under-development of Africa, after centuries of colonial domination, was not due to any lack of intelligence among the colonizers; on the other hand, the development of Africa, which would have to take place immediately, would depend on whether Africans had the requisite intelligence. Of course, by raising the question, Cryns left no doubt of his answer. Still, he did not allow matters to rest there, but turned instead to the racial comparisons of "intelligence" made during the colonial era.

In reading Cryns and others on this subject, one learns the following: The first mental tests on the African continent were administered in South Africa in 1915, when one A.L. Martin gave the Binet to African youths and children. He came to two conclusions: that the testees were deficient in the requirements for "abstract thought," and that the Binet should be revised for use on "uncivilised children and adults." In 1929, the precedent for mass IQ testing in South Africa was set when comparisons were made between the test scores of 10,000 black, Indian, "coloured," and white children. In this same decade, several testing projects were also conducted to support a biological-determinist thesis known as "early arrest," which holds that an African's mental development stops earlier than that of a white, making an African adult the mental equivalent of a white child.

Starting with the 1930s and continuing through the balance of the colonial period, the Portuguese, British, French, Belgians, and Spanish conducted IQ tests in their respective colonies. The Portuguese tested Mozambicans, using Portuguese soldiers as the "control group," or standard of comparison. The British tested Kenyan schoolboys and compared their scores with those of English schoolboys. The Belgians tested Congolese miners and other groups of Congolese adults, and—reflecting the influence of the early-arrest notion—used Belgian schoolchildren's scores as the standard.

In French Sudan (as Mali was then called), Senegal, and Guinea, the French tested Africans of various age groups; they used French three-year-olds as the standard of comparison for African adults and teenagers. And a team of Americans (including a Yale psychobiologist), who went to Guinea in the early 1930s to study chimpanzees, also administered tests to the human population. In their report on the testing project (which was apparently one of the earliest conducted in Africa by Americans), they expressed appreciation to the French colonial government for making the study possible.

In the 1930s some testers also compared Africans on the basis of sex, predictably using the data to uphold the claim of a relationship between gender and intelligence. The tests in Africa also provided much grist for the nature-nurture argument. At first the scores were interpreted only from a hereditarian standpoint, but by the 1930s they had also been reinterpreted from an environmentalist stance.

In his article titled "African Intelligence" (1962) Cryns not only discussed the psychometricians' activities in Africa but also those of the craniologists. Although the latter had virtually passed from the scene in Europe and the United States by the end of the nineteenth century, they were active in Africa into the 1950s. As result, the skulls and brains of deceased Africans were subjected to physical tests at the same time living Africans were subjected to mental ones.[4]

As for the outcome of Cryns' mission, having set out to determine whether Africans have the intelligence to lead the countries they had liberated from those deemed their mental superiors (a point he neglected to mention), he found himself in agreement both with the psychometricians who claim that Africans lack the ability to abstract and the craniometricians who claim that Africans have less developed brains.

II

In recent years the number of testing projects in Africa has increased enormously. A far greater number were conducted in countries of sub-Saharan Africa between 1960 and 1975 than during the preceding two hundred years. While part of the increase is due to the fact that the psychometricians still have far more than a foot in the door in certain Third-World countries, the major reason lies elsewhere, in the tests conducted in South Africa by the National Institute for Personnel Research (NIPR) of the South African Council for Scientific and Industrial Research.[5] By its own count, the NIPR has tested "literally millions of Africans."[6]

The NIPR was established in 1948, the year that the Afrikaners, with their doctrine of apartheid, came to power. Their takeover did not mark a departure from but rather an intensification of the dominant ideology and practices in South Africa. "Racism certainly did not see the light of day in South Africa only in 1948 when the Afrikaner nationalists . . . won a shock victory . . . with their unashamed doctrine of *baaskap* (overlordship), of keeping the black man in his place," pointed out Archbishop Desmond M. Tutu.[7]

Discussing the historical conditions in which apartheid emerged—and the role of IQ tests in justifying it—Archbishop Tutu stressed the "central racist ideology of the Afrikaner people,

> according to which, following much that was current as science in the West, and following in the wake of a burgeoning white imperialism that rode roughshod over colonial peoples, white people were inherently superior to black people. After all, this had been claimed by the taxonomical studies that spoke mystifyingly about the brain and cranium size and subsequently about the psychological evidence deriving from IQ tests, etc.[8]

Archbishop Tutu stressed that not only the Afrikaners have

been "guilty of such supremacist views," but the "so-called liberal English-speaking South African" has also "tended to hold such views." Members of that group, however, have been "careful not to be as blatant in their expression as the less subtle Afrikaner."[9]

In examining the NIPR's ideological stance, one finds that it corresponds (at least in those of its pronouncements that reach the West) to the approach favored by the English-speaking whites. For example, at its founding the NIPR avoided identification with blatantly biological-determinist views, and sought to develop a predominantly environmentalist image. It had a most practical reason for doing so. Had the NIPR, as an adjunct of the apartheid state, openly associated itself with hereditarianism in the post–World War II period, when the Nazis' use of this doctrine was still fresh in people's minds, it would have created a barrier to the acceptance it sought (and quite readily won) from some Western academic circles.

The NIPR's environmentalist image was established primarily through the writing of its founding director, Simon Biesheuval. In 1949, in an article treated by cross-cultural psychometricians as a classic environmentalist interpretation of the colonial-era tests, he used a cultural-deprivation thesis to explain the assumed racial intelligence differentials. At the same time, however, he left the way open to the possibility of a genetic component.[10] Then, in an article published the same year as Jensen's, he readjusted his emphasis and placed the genetic interpretation on an equal footing with the environmentalist one.[11]

In using both social and genetic concepts to justify the claim of black mental inferiority, Biesheuval followed in the footsteps of South Africa's "theoreticians of racism." Oliver Tambo, president of the African National Congress—in a speech made when he accepted an award, in 1986, on behalf of Nelson and Winnie Mandela—observed:

> The theoreticians of racism in our country drew on the gross
> perversions of science which assumed their clearest forms

during the second half of the last century in Europe and the
United States. In these centres of imperialist power there
grew up theories that biology and social anthropology provided the basis to justify the notion that all Black people
carried with them both an innate and a cultural inferiority
to the White, giving the latter the right and duty of guard-
ianship over the former.[12]

Apartheid's Tests

The NIPR has carried out two basic types of activity. One
involves testing Africans that NIPR officials openly label "primitive." David J.M. Vorster, Biesheuval's successor, professed scientific motives for carrying on this traditional, racist endeavor:
"Studies of isolated groups of primitive people can contribute
toward a better understanding of the development of cognitive
functions in man."[13]

The organization's other—and major—activity is suggested
by the word "personnel" in its title: job-related testing. The
NIPR's procedure in this area differs from that of Western
psychometricians. While the latter give the same tests to different racial groups, and rely upon the tests' covert bias to sort the
testees in the desired manner, the NIPR makes no such pre-
tenses: it gives different tests to different races. It uses, for
example, a whites-only test for selecting scientists and blacks-
only tests for the "placement and utilization of laborers."[14]

The NIPR has had a general program for testing black industrial workers. In addition, it has conducted special testing projects in almost every industry, but in particular among the gold
and copper miners. The reports on these projects are usually
labeled "confidential." But it is evident even from the minimal
information the NIPR does release on these projects, as well as
from its nonconfidential reports, that the testing program's
central objective is to assist the apartheid state in maintaining
control.

The NIPR designed tests to rank blacks according to their
attitudes to "authority and the work situation."[15] To carry out

this mission, the tests were constructed with a feature that originated with IQ tests, i.e., the use of items that require agreement with designated social values. The NIPR also uses a test, the Modern-Traditional Scale, that serves the related purpose of ranking test takers on the basis of ideas deemed modern by the upholders of apartheid. The test, which was designed by Biesheuval, has also been adapted by Western psychometricians for use in Third-World countries.

Despite their preoccupation with testing the attitudes of blacks, South African psychometricians have displayed little confidence in the results. As early as 1958, Biesheuval warned of the "difficulty" in "ensuring that the verbalised attitudes" reflect the blacks' "actual beliefs."[16] If he was warning the authorities that they should not take apparently reassuring results at face value, it was because of the "hostility" he had already encountered.

> The uneducated non-European has very little notion of what testing is all about, and those who are educated know only too well from past experience that conclusions unfavourable to their racial or cultural group are likely to be drawn from their findings. This produces attitudes varying from outright hostility and refusal to do the tests, to going through the motions without making much effort.[17]

Thus Biesheuval admitted that blacks in South Africa have long defied the mental testers. Not surprisingly, he also distorted his admission by presuming that only educated blacks would do so. Such presumptions were due to be severely jolted by the role uneducated blacks would play, along with educated ones, in events that were to come.

III

Given Cryns' agreement with the claims of both the psychometricians and the craniometricians, it may seem surprising that he subtitled his article "A *Critical* Survey of Cross-Cultural Intelligence Research in Africa South of the Sahara" (emphasis added). And it may seem even more surprising that the article was perceived in the field as a critical one, with Cole, for example, declaring, "The excessive claims of the intelligence testers have been adequately criticized by Cryns."[18]

How could it be said that Cryns criticized the early testers' claims as excessive, when he had reiterated their claims? The answer is that he agreed with them that Africans are inferior in intelligence, but felt they went astray by treating the tests, as he put it, as universal measures, when they should instead have recognized the "cultural specificity" of intelligence and so treated the tests as Western yardsticks.[19] While Cryns' criticism seems abstruse, it refers to a practical matter: the early testers' use in Africa of the same tests used in the West, which left their *modus operandi* excessively vulnerable to charges of cultural bias.

Cryns' article reflected the testers' increasing concern with using tests that would appear to be appropriate for the populations tested. The product of this concern has been a proliferation of tests constructed for a particular region (e.g., the Pacific Reasoning Test), a particular country (e.g., the Sierra Leone Test), or even a particular testing expedition. Each of these tests is designed for one of two basic uses.

In one usage, the same test is given to an indigenous population and to a control group whose members are either European or of European descent; the test is claimed to be suitable for both groups. In the other usage, different tests, which are described as "conceptually equivalent," are given to the indigenous group and the control group.

Whichever technique is used, however, the tests' bias remains intact. Where the same test is used for both populations, the Western bias is obvious. Where a special test is devised for each population, the bias is more deceptive. For example, a test for an African population may contain references familiar to that culture, but it will also call for formal-logical skills that the group has either had no opportunity or a lesser opportunity to acquire than the Western control group. Because the tests are simply projections of the IQ method, which equates formal logical skills with the human ability to reason, they uniformly yield data to support the claim that Third-World populations are deficient in the ability to abstract.

Commenting on the cross-cultural tests given over the years, Cole stated, "The almost universal outcome of the psychological study of culture and cognition has been the demonstration of large differences among cultural groups on a large variety of psychological tests. . . . This has led to the widespread belief that different cultures produce different [cognitive] processes."[20]

Cole has turned matters around. Contrary to his assertion, the outcome of mental tests has not "led to" the belief that different cultures produce different/unequal cognitive processes, but preceded it. It is because this prior assumption is built into the tests that the tests churn out data in support of the assumption.

Cole also reversed matters in another way: "The major challenge for cognitive research is to design experiments that yield measures of the processes giving rise to performance and that rule out at least the most plausible rival hypotheses about the processes involved."[21] But psychometric techniques do not rule out rival hypotheses. On the contrary, mental measurement helps to sustain a variety of them, including many that antedated it—and that might have disappeared had this pseudo-science not lent them an aura of plausibility.

It is because the tests cannot measure conceptualized processes, and instead measure or test performances designated as their surrogates, that they help keep rival hypotheses afloat. However, these rival speculations not only vie for acceptance, they also share a basic feature, i.e., they seek explanations for group differences in performance in non-observable processes, while overlooking such demonstrable phenomena as test bias.

Rationale for Repetition

Since the outcome of the immense number of cross-cultural tests conducted over many decades has virtually always been the same, what reason do the testers give for continuing them? The tests are conducted, they say, to develop theories on cognition for use in both the Third World and the United States—for example, to solve educational problems for Third-World populations and for "subcultural" groups at home.

This explanation raises a question: why travel to the Third World to solve educational problems for minorities at home? The answer lies in the testers' belief that the problems do not stem from unequal education but from cognitive deficits or differences, and that these can be better understood by studying what they call either "primitive" or "traditional" peoples.

Suggesting the link between the testers' theories and their practical objectives, Cole stated, "If our data support theories that have predictive power, the result, although not perfect for all purposes, can be considered useful."[22] Thus Cole slightly recast a standard rationale for IQ tests: they may not be perfect but their predictive power makes them useful—e.g., for tracking.

In Third-World countries, tests are used to make predictions analogous to those made at home. Biesheuval, displaying a keen interest in these countries, wrote, "Pressure for the rapid advancement of the indigenous populations . . . compelled the sorting out of those who could make the best use of available opportunities. Measuring devices of proved validity in Western contexts generally required substantial modification . . . for effective prediction in different cultures."[23]

Of course, the modified tests make the same predictions that are built into the original tests, namely, that the "best use" of available opportunities will be made by those whose socioeconomic status is higher. Thus the tests designed for Third-World use help preserve the stratification imposed by colonialism.

To see how a concept created by cross-cultural researchers is applied both to Africans and African-Americans, let us turn to Bruner. In 1971, Bruner revived the early-arrest thesis, which had been introduced by biological determinists. Reinterpreting this notion from a cultural-determinist standpoint, he stated,

As Werner (1948) pointed out, "Development among primi-

tive people is characterized [. . .] by a relatively early arrest
of the process of intellectual growth." . . . [Unschooled
children] stabilize earlier and do not go on to new levels of
operation. The same "early arrest" characterizes the differences between "culturally deprived" and other American
children.[24]

On the one hand, this thesis attributes the alleged early arrest
of mental development in African children to an absence of
schooling and, on the other, attributes the same presumed
condition in African-American children to cultural deprivation.
Since the thesis holds that Africans or people of African descent
suffer for one reason or another from stunted cognition, it
justifies the "early arrest" of education for African-Americans
and its continued denial to Africans.

IV

As one cross-cultural researcher admitted, the "invasion by
foreign researchers" of the Third World is viewed there as a
"more or less subtle form of exploitation." This view of Western
researchers can be explained by, among other reasons, the fact
that they have produced a plethora of works misinterpreting the
causes of underdevelopment. Walter Rodney, the Guyanese historian and author of *How Europe Underdeveloped Africa* (1972),
commented on the source of the misinterpretations: "Mistaken
interpretations of the causes of underdevelopment usually stem
either from prejudiced thinking or from the error of believing
that one can learn the answers by looking inside the underdeveloped economy."[25]

The assumption that the populations of underdeveloped countries are underdeveloped in intelligence is at the core of the belief
that the causes of underdevelopment can be found within an
underdeveloped country. This misinterpretation is so prevalent,
noted Rodney, that it has often been thought best to avoid even
the proper use of "underdeveloped": "In some quarters, it has
often been thought wise to substitute the term 'developing' for

'underdeveloped.' One of the reasons for so doing is to avoid any unpleasantness which may be attached to the second term, which might be interpreted as meaning underdeveloped mentally."[26]

The Forerunners

When the colonialists' notion that the colonized peoples were underdeveloped mentally was converted into "science," the anthropologists played a special role. Take, for example, the British empire's preeminent anthropologist, Edward Burnett Tylor.

Tylor, the author of *Primitive Culture* (1871), believed it was the colonialists' mission to bring higher or "universal" standards to those they assumed were at a lower stage on the evolutionary scale. Setting a precedent for the psychometricians, Tylor proceeded on the assumption that a population's level of intelligence correlates with the society's level of scientific and technological development. He held that an "excellent guide" to the "relation of the mental condition of savages to that of civilized men" is the "development of the material arts."[27]

Tylor did not go to the colonies himself, but relied on the accounts of missionaries and travelers. Although his method did not yield the "measured arithmetical facts of modern statistics," he nonetheless felt sure his conclusions would "bear comparison with the statisticians' returns," had such been available.[28] As it turned out, this was quite true, although hardly surprising. That Tylor's conclusions tally with those of the psychometricians simply reflects that the latter's methods incorporate, albeit covertly, the same prior assumptions.

An affinity also exists between the mental testers' concepts and those of Lucien Lévy-Bruhl, the French anthropologist and author of *Les Fonctions Mentales Dans Les Sociétés Inférieures* (1910). Like Tylor, Lévy-Bruhl remained in the "mother country" and depended on the accounts of missionaries, etc. He made no effort to create an illusion of distance between his work and the colonialists' concerns; he published his thanks to the colonial administrators who were "good enough to write and tell me that [my] volumes have been of service to them."[29] The service for which the colonialists were particularly grateful was his classification of the mental processes of the colonized as "prelogical."

"We Are Often Charged . . ."

The essence of Lévy-Bruhl's thesis — that certain populations are deficient in logical abilities — is at the core of the IQ method. Hence the revised tests in use today make the contemporary cross-cultural testers as vulnerable to criticism as their predecessors. This vulnerability is evident in a disclaimer offered by two leading cross-cultural testers, whose remarks are notable for, shall we say, their testiness: "Comparative cognitive psychological research is *not* aimed at discovering which peoples are clever, smart, or intelligent, and which are not; we are often charged with this aim by critics of testing and supporters of minority group rights."[30]

Unsurprisingly, this statement distorts the views of testing's opponents, who do not charge that cross-cultural tests are aimed at *discovering* which peoples are intelligent and which are not, but are aimed instead at *supporting* the prior assumption that certain peoples are intelligent and others are not.

In their efforts to rebut charges of bias, the cross-cultural testers follow the same procedure as their domestic counterparts. They use revised tests accompanied by revised theses. Among the most influential of the latter is the cognitive-differences concept, whose forebears include a position that emerged from the field of anthropology: "cultural relativism." Commenting on this view, Gould stated: "[T]hroughout the egalitarian tradition of the European Enlightenment and the American revolution, I cannot identify any popular position remotely like the 'cultural relativism' that prevails (at least by lip-service) in liberal circles today."[31]

No doubt the reason Gould could not find a historical precedent for cultural relativism is that it emerged arbitrarily, during the latter phase of colonialism, as a position designed to serve pragmatic purposes. Although he was incorrect in suggesting that its adherents are limited to liberal circles, he was certainly accurate in saying that it prevails by lip-service. In fact, it cannot be observed in any other way.

According to its supporters, cultural relativism is a value-free or nonbiased position that considers each society's values or standards valid for that society. When it was introduced its supporters portrayed it, on the one hand, as the answer to the colonialists' claims that they were the bearers of universal values and, on the other, as a position that respects the cultures of the colonized. But in reality, cultural relativism was a means for giving lip-service to respect for the latter's cultures. As a position that maintains *all* value systems should be respected, it legitimated the values of the dominant group, the colonialists, who continued to do what they had done for centuries, that is, destroy the cultures of the colonized.

Since cultural relativism claims to make no value judgments, it has been used to justify underdevelopment as a way of life appropriate to peoples living in underdeveloped societies. At the same time, cultural relativism holds that different social conditions produce different ways of reasoning, thus placing the onus for underdevelopment on the peoples who were colonized. In other words, it makes the erroneous assumption that the causes of underdevelopment can be found by "looking inside the under-developed country."

Although cultural relativism is highly influential among cross-cultural researchers, Cole chastised them (particularly those who carry out their work in this country) for not adopting this position: "[T]he cultures being compared are rarely considered different but equal."[32] By maintaining that all cultures should be considered equal, Cole appeared to criticize biased or ethno-centric approaches. But the point is not that all cultures are equal, since they clearly are not. (How, for instance, is it possible to equate the racist culture of the white South African minority with the antiracist culture of the black majority?) The point is that the thought processes of all people are equal, i.e., that cognitive processes are universal.

But while cross-cultural psychologists may or may not assert cultural equality, the results of cross-cultural tests (as Cole has acknowledged) overwhelmingly deny cognitive equality. Cole himself proposed a guide to future research that would assure more of the same results: "[T]he concept of *functional cognitive systems*, which may vary with cultural variations, may be a most useful approach to guide future research and may at some point offer the possibility of an eventual integration of theory and fact in this field."[33]

Cole made the striking admission that facts have never been found to uphold the old a priori assumption that different cultures produce different cognitive processes. Yet he nonetheless proposed that this assumption continue to guide cross-cultural research.

The belief that different cultures produce different cognitive systems has already guided the work of a remarkable number of individuals. For example, according to a contemporary writer who has revived Lévy-Bruhl's work and redefined it as "cognitive relativism," his concepts were forerunners of the cognitive-differences thesis.[34] Of course, it can just as easily be argued that they were forerunners of the cognitive-deficit thesis, but this merely reflects the affinity between the deficit and differences position.[35] While the latter view is likely to be presented in a more subtle fashion, both positions maintain that—because of differentials in the ability to abstract—some populations have cognitive processes suitable for functioning in technologically advanced societies and others do not.

"Common to Whole of Humanity"

Because psychometrics is a pseudoscience, one psychometrician never offers a substantive challenge to another. But this is not true of anthropologists per se. In this country in 1911, for example, Franz Boas published *The Mind of Primitive Man*. Contrary to the impression his title creates, the book represents a fundamental break with the Lévy-Bruhl–type position.

Boas opposed the claim that different peoples have different cognitive processes; he held that the "functions of the human mind are common to the whole of humanity."[36] Making an acute distinction between what is and what is not affected by socio-cultural factors, he held that different cultural phenomena affect *what* different peoples think, i.e., their attitudes or psychology, but not the *way* they think, i.e., their processes of thought: "[S]ocial conditions, on account of their peculiar characteristics, easily convey the impression that the mind of primitive man acts in a way quite different from ours, while in reality the fundamental traits of the mind are the same."[37]

While he used the phrase "primitive man," Boas offered proofs that controvert the myth of primitive mind. He did this in two ways. On the one hand, he showed the universality of thought processes, taking language as one of his proofs. Every people has a "well-organized language,"[38] and every language has "similar traits."[39] At the same time, he demonstrated that the primitive-mind assumption is the product of bias: European and Euro-American observers misinterpreted the reactions of indigenous peoples, and then took their own misinterpretations as evidence of the mental inferiority of those they observed.

The Mind of Primitive Man is distinguished by its advanced thesis. That it also contains weaknesses and contrarieties, as do Boas' later writings, does not alter the fact that his contribution is outstanding. From his early through his final work he affirmed and reaffirmed that all human populations possess a common cognitive process.

One gauge of the influence of his work is that Lévy-Bruhl, shortly before his death, renounced his "prelogical" concept. In a reiteration of Boas' thesis, he stated, "The logical structure of the mind is the same in all known human societies, just as they all have a language, customs and institutions; accordingly, to speak no longer of the 'prelogical' character."[40] Although the retraction was not as unequivocal as it appears to be (he went on to make certain qualifications), it is—in view of the influence of his original claim—highly significant.

V

Returning to Gould, we find that he quite bluntly reasserted Tylor's old correlation of a people's level of intelligence with the society's level of technological development. He stated that "complex culture requires a certain level of intelligence."[41] By using the phrase "complex culture," Gould implied the existence of its opposite, simple or "primitive" culture—an assumption controverted by the complexity of all languages, as well as by many scientific determinations about early societies.

Making the equation between a society's level of development and its population's level of intelligence in yet another way— while also suggesting that he is expressing the latest scientific consensus—Gould stated, "We now believe that different attitudes and styles of thought among human groups are usually the nongenetic products of cultural evolution."[42]

Gould confused the effects of cultural evolution. While different sociocultural conditions produce different attitudes, they do not (as Boas showed) produce different styles of thought, i.e., different cognitive processes.

When Gould stated that different styles of thought are usually the nongenetic products of cultural evolution, he implied that the claimed differences may sometimes be biological in origin. While leaving an opening to the genetic interpretation is (as we have shown) quite common among environmentalists, one aspect of Gould's approach was rather unusual. By speaking of different styles of thought, Gould seemed to express the cultural-differences concept. But this concept, as an offshoot of cultural relativism, does not recognize cultural evolution. Thus he apparently borrowed the terminology of one thesis to express another, i.e., the cognitive-deficit concept, which recognizes cultural evolution only to distort its effects.

On a deeper level, however, Gould's composite concept once again reveals that, given the absence of a substantive difference between them, any distinction between the differences and deficits concepts can be no more than a matter of semantics.

VI

In his last chapter, Lawler included a brief denunciation of colonialism. This was an ironic touch because it was preceded by a reiteration of the claims of colonialism's anthropologists. Lawler offered, for example, a variation of Lévy-Bruhl's claim that the colonized peoples were prelogical by speaking of a "historical evolution from preliterate to literate methods of thought" and the "preliterate oral culture of primitive peoples."[43]

Presenting the notion that peoples in underdeveloped countries are underdeveloped in intelligence in terms peculiarly evocative of earlier centuries — when biologists and others did not hesitate to compare certain human groups with nonhuman ones — Lawler wrote: "From an historical point of view, we see . . . enormous advances in real intellectual and practical capacities rooted in modern industry and science. Such real capacities cannot be found by scrutinizing the 'naked ape' stripped of all the instruments of knowledge and practice that make human beings to be truly human."[44]

The phrase "naked ape" comes from the book of the same name, whose author, a zoologist and biological determinist, used it to describe the human species.[45] As is apparent, Lawler did not reject the naked-ape notion, but instead adapted it: as he saw it, populations in countries with advanced science and industry — in contrast to those in Third-World countries — have evolved beyond the "primitive" and become "truly human."

In presenting this familiar view, Lawler seemed to introduce a novel touch. Apparently treating science and industry as the source of human characteristics, he saw "intellectual capacities" (another of the psychometricians' synonyms for "intelligence") as rooted in technology. In essence, however, he was simply expressing the claimed correlation between level of technology and level of intelligence in a rather unusual way.

Lawler also proposed a test that is an overt expression of this correlation.

"Absolute" Measure

Along with various psychometricians, Lawler held that IQ tests measure intelligence relatively, that is, by ranking test takers against an average score. Although he accepted this method, he also believed it should be improved upon. To this end, he proposed a method that would, by his own description, go beyond IQ tests by replacing their relative standard with an "absolute" or "real" one.

Although IQ tests were created to circumvent the craniologists' failure to find a real, i.e., physical, measure of intelligence, Lawler maintained that his proposed measure, while not physical, is nonetheless real: a "real measure of intelligence" consists of "actual knowledge and skills, including scientific theory."[46] He asserted that his test could be used, for example, to measure "algebraic capacity."[47]

Since Lawler's test also takes scholastically acquired skills and knowledge as its measure of intelligence, it would join IQ tests as a means for justifying a social status quo in which access to education is unequal along class and racial lines. Of course, his test is unlikely to be put into use since it is an unsubtle variant of IQ tests, which take school performance as their *covert* measure of intelligence. In any event, Lawler did not see his test as a substitute for but a supplement to IQ tests, which he invested with many attributes. In a particularly telling example of this point, he wrote, "The fact that not all cultures do score well on [IQ] tests is an important point that has profound implications for a scientific understanding of the development of 'intelligence' understood as involving formal logical operations."[48]

Thus Lawler took the reductionist approach that obliterates

the distinction between formal logic and the human ability to think logically, to reason. But it is the fact that all peoples possess this ability, and not the results of pseudoscientific tests, that has profound implications for a scientific understanding of human mental processes.

Given the opportunity to acquire formal logical skills, human beings do so. But formal logic does not subsume the creativity, flexibility, or other qualities of human consciousness. As a result, it plays a limited, albeit important, role. It is, for instance, a valuable method for analyzing established knowledge and theories. Yet because its rules are rigid, one can follow them without arriving at any aspect of the truth. Thus, long before it was incorporated into IQ tests, the precedent for using formal logic to uphold false, racist claims had been set.

"Logic was manipulated to give intellectual credence to the system of slavery," pointed out Martin Luther King, Jr. "Someone formulated the argument for the inferiority of the Negro in the shape of a syllogism":

> All men are made in the image of God;
> God, as everybody knows, is not a Negro;
> Therefore, the Negro is not a man.[49]

VII

At the same time that the psychometricians conduct tests whose "almost universal outcome" supports the myth of Western mind–primitive mind, they ignore or, when that is impossible, deny the *real* evidence of a universal cognitive process. There are many separate proofs of this universality, but there is also an all-embracing one: had the colonized been of unequal intelligence, they could never have liberated themselves from the colonizers.

Because the colonialists assumed their own mental superiority, history caught them by surprise. Take the Portuguese. "[T]he Portuguese did not know the African, even though they came from the European country with the most colonies in Africa," observed Amilcar Cabral, who led Guinea-Bissau's liberation struggle and headed that nation after independence was won. "Thus, as a result of our struggle, as a result of our confrontation with the Portuguese, they realised that we were not what they had supposed, and they discovered an African they had never imagined. This was one of the surprises the enemy got from our struggle."[50]

Such was the outcome of a conflict in which one side came to know the other only too well, while the other was blinded by its belief in a myth of its own creation.

Inventing "Primitivism"

When the myth of Western mind–primitive mind was put into "scholarly" form, one of the names it acquired was "primitivism." Ekpo Eyo, director of Nigeria's Commission for Museums and Monuments, has noted:

> From the moment when Europeans and North Americans adopted the concept of civilization for themselves, all others had to be regarded as uncivilized or primitive. And in the attempts of Western scholars to justify this claim to superiority, they invented the notion of primitivism and spread it wherever their influence reached.[51]

To maintain the myth of primitivism/primitive mind, the colonialists engaged in lies and distortions and, when all else failed, simply shifted from one claim to another. As one example of this syndrome, which did not end with colonialism, let us take the incident involving the theft of ancient Nigerian art.

After the British violently invaded Benin in 1897, their booty included some two thousand magnificent bronzes (which they sold to pay the cost of the expedition). "Cellini could not have cast them better. Nor could anyone else, before or after Cellini," declared an authority on art in the early part of this century.[52] Today, most of these bronzes are still to be found in British and other Western museums.

Since the British colonialists "knew" that Africans could not have developed the art of bronze casting, they decided the Benin sculptors had learned it from the Portuguese, who had arrived in Benin near the end of the fifteenth century. There was, as it turned out, a problem with this attribution. At the time the African sculptors were suppposed to have learned casting from the Portuguese, the Portuguese themselves had not yet learned to cast.

That this particular claim had to be abandoned did not mean that the effort to derogate ancient Nigeria's art had to be jettisoned. On the contrary, the colonialists could simply shift to other claims, because they had already denigrated the sculptures as products of a primitive mentality.

Myths and Math

If Lawler's proposed test of "algebraic capacity" were put into use, it would "find" this hypothetical trait only in those populations with access to a good education in mathematics. Thus it would join a host of other IQ-type tests in sustaining a special facet of the primitive-mind myth, that Africans, because of an inability to abstract, are devoid of mathematical capacities.

Contrary to the myth, however, Africans have developed many mathematical systems, whose existence—like innumerable other aspects of African reality—have been hidden or distorted. The Yoruba, for example, developed a system that is a "fascinating chapter in the history of mathematics," pointed out Robert G. Armstrong, author of *Yoruba Numerals* (1962).[53] "It is testimony to the Yoruba capacity for abstract reasoning that they could have developed and learned such a system."[54]

One of the few books in English that deal with African mathematical systems is *The Number Concept* (1896) by L.L. Conant. "Conant's point of view is completely colored by the prevailing attitude toward Africans as 'primitive savages'; they were deemed hardly human," observed Claudia Zaslavsky, author of *Africa Counts* (1979). Conant, whose influence persists, "dismisses the amazingly complex numeration system of the Yoruba people."[55]

One of Conant's means for dismissing this system was his use of semantics. When, for example, Yorubas performed what he described as "unexpected feats of reckoning," he attributed it to "continued use of the trading and bargaining faculties."[56] Although it is certainly true (as Zaslavsky shows) that mathematical systems were developed in socioeconomic contexts, this was hardly Conant's point. Having found "unexpected" mathematical ability in Africans, he tried to explain it away by substituting "trading and bargaining faculties" for what he would have called "faculties of abstraction" in Europeans or Euro-Americans.

Shifting Tides

The stratagem of shifting grounds — of introducing an adjusted claim when a prior one has been exposed — made a great impression on W.E.B. Du Bois. "The first thing which brought me to my senses in all this racial discussion was the continuous change in the proofs and arguments advanced," recalled Du Bois, who not only saw claims about evolution, culture, skull measurements, and IQ tests advanced as incontrovertible proofs of African-American inferiority, but also saw all of these claims controverted.[57]

One particularly long-running episode in the history of the shifting-grounds stratagem began during the colonial era, when Europeans reported that they had witnessed amazing feats of navigation by "primitive" peoples. Since it would have been unthinkable to attribute these feats to mental abilities, they resorted to other explanations. One of Lévy-Bruhl's sources ascribed the feats to an "innate faculty," something akin, it would seem, to the migratory instinct in birds. Although he by no means dismissed this interpretation, Lévy-Bruhl himself (in comments made before his recantation) fell back on another old favorite: "with them memory takes the place of . . . operations which elsewhere depend upon a logical process."[58]

Matters stood at this point until the late 1960s, when Thomas Gladwin, an anthropologist, studied the legendary navigators of Puluwat, an island in the western Pacific, with the aim of attaining "insight" into the academic problems of poor children in the United States. Explaining why he sought this insight on a distant island, he provided the following model of formal logic. Poor American children generally do "badly" on IQ tests, and the same could be expected of Puluwatans; therefore the cognitive qualities that "handicap" poor children could be discovered in the Puluwatans.[59] These handicaps, he believed, would be revealed by comparing the way Puluwatans plan their voyages with the way Western navigators plan theirs.[60]

Gladwin's conclusions from his research confounded his a priori assumptions. The Puluwat system is "complex, rational, efficient."[61] Not only does it involve an organized body of knowledge, but it is based on a *body of theory*. Although Puluwat navigation calls for a vast knowledge of star sequences, it is not taught by rote but as a "logically coherent system."[62] As to the presumed differences in the way Puluwatans plan their voyages: their approach is superficially different from that of Western navigators, but they "cover the same things for the same reasons."[63]

With his assumptions about Puluwat mental processes in a state of collapse, Gladwin considered the implications: there is reason to "suspect the validity" of the "one distinction" on which there is "considerable agreement," i.e., the belief that middle-class children engage in abstract thought, while poor children are limited to the concrete.[64]

Having felt compelled to suspect this belief, Gladwin should have suspected another: that poor children's cognitive processes handicap their academic performance. This in turn would logically have led him to suspect that the handicap lies elsewhere, i.e., in schools that provide superior and inferior education along class and racial lines. But rather than pursue a logical course, he pursued the illogical but traditional one described by Du Bois. Substituting one claim for another, he speculated as to whether there might not be yet another cognitive peculiarity that handicaps poor children.

VIII

The cross-cultural researchers who go to the Third World to develop concepts for use at home have somehow overlooked one whose universality is attested by a vast amount of evidence. This concept—which may be inferred from Cabral's observation about the Portuguese colonialists' failure to know the Africans—is that those who deem themselves superior cannot know those they deem inferior, while the latter can and do come to know the former.

The applicability of this concept to the United States becomes evident when one considers the African-American experience. Take, for example, the slavery period. The masters, certain they knew their slaves well, assumed that the blacks could not abstract, had only a rudimentary grasp of language, etc. But at the very time the masters were making assumptions about blacks that still prevail, the slaves were engaged in a subtle and complex process of thought and communication beyond the grasp of their masters. John Lovell, Jr., a historian, wrote: "[T]he [black slave] *analyzed* and *synthesized* his life in his songs and sayings. In hundreds of songs called spirituals, he produced an epic cycle; and, as in each such instance, he concealed there his deepest thoughts and ideas, his hard-finished plans and hopes and dreams" (emphasis added).[65]

The complexity of the spirituals lies in their duality; they communicated certain ideas and plans to the slaves while concealing them from the masters. To do this, they used two products of abstraction, mask and symbol. "Many people honestly do not believe that the spirituals use mask and symbolism," noted Lovell. He pointed out that the Biblical figures in the spirituals—Moses, Jesus, Daniel, David, Joshua—served as masks so far as the masters were concerned, while the same figures—who were "involved in upheaval and revolution"— served as symbols for the slaves.[66]

Take "Steal Away to Jesus." Because the slaves followed "Steal away" with "to Jesus," the master, "always close by, is satisfied that this is a purely religious enterprise; his suspicion, aroused by the first 'Steal away,' is fully allayed." But the "slave poet goes on":

> Steal away, steal away home,
> I ain't got long to stay here![67]

Yet even at this point, the masters did not see beyond the mask. They never "knew (or believed) that the slave had already made contact with a representative of the Underground Railroad." But the slaves "knew well the implications" of the song's first verse.

> My Lord calls me, He calls me by the thunder;
> The Trumpet sounds within-a-my soul,
> I ain't got long to stay here![68]

Finally, the slaves themselves tore away the mask, compelling the masters to recognize the message, if not the symbolism, of the spirituals.

> Of course, the chariot in "Swing Low" is some arm of freedom reaching out to draw [the slave] in; and the number of times it succeeded shows that it was no hopeless hope. Of course, "My Lord delibered Daniel . . . why can't he deliber me" means just what it says . . . . And the falling rocks and mountains hit the slave's enemies. You would never get the communities all over the South which tasted slave revolts . . . to believe that these rocks and mountains were ethereal, or that they couldn't fall at any time . . . . The slave song was an awesome prophecy rooted in the knowledge of what was going on.[69]

The spirituals expressed many facets of the slaves' hopes, including their deep desire for education. During Reconstruction, the former slaves led in electing the black and white legislators who provided the legal basis for education in the South, where 75 percent of the non-slaveholding whites were also nonliterate. With the undoing of Reconstruction, and the imposition of segregation, these laws were overturned and replaced by legislation mandating separate and unequal education.

As part of the process of reversing Reconstruction, the southern states introduced tests for voters. Although ostensibly intended for all prospective voters, they were given only to blacks; whites were exempted by such circumventions as the "grandfather clause." "[B]lacks were disfranchised by the use of 'tests'. . . . [T]esting helped weave the racist fabric of the United States," observed the *NAACP Report on Minority Testing.*[70]

Like the slave South, the post-Reconstruction South had its academically trained spokesmen with formal-logical arguments at their disposal. Yet, as Du Bois pointed out in 1903, the blacks' "counter-cries, lacking though they may be in formal logic, have burning truths within them."[71]

It would not be long before Du Bois would become the first major opponent of the IQ test, the device that obliterates the distinction between formal logic and human reasoning ability — and so allows the old claim of racial and class intelligence differentials to be "validated" in a more sophisticated way in the twentieth century than was feasible in earlier times.

The Risk Factor

I

"Millions of this nation's children are at risk" from schools that do not offer them an equal chance to learn. This is the message of *Barriers to Excellence: Our Children at Risk*.[1] This major study was published in 1985, two years after publication of *A Nation at Risk*, a report that reversed the risk.

According to *A Nation at Risk*, which had been commissioned by Secretary of Education T.H. Bell, the problem is not that the nation is putting children at risk, but that children are putting the nation at risk. In a remark that was destined for the media, *A Nation at Risk* warned: "[T]he educational foundations of our society are presently being eroded by a rising tide of mediocrity that threatens our very future as a Nation and a people."[2]

The warning has a familiar ring. No wonder. It recalls the post–World War I alarm over a "decline of American intelligence." Like its predecessor, the alarm was set off by a report on test scores. Thus the onus for the "rising tide of mediocrity" fell on children with lower scores on contemporary tests, just as the onus for the "decline of American intelligence" had fallen on draftees with lower scores on the WWI tests.

After the Decline

To support its claim of a "rising tide of mediocrity," *A Nation at Risk* treated the test-score decline as an ongoing phenomenon. But the evidence shows that test scores in general had begun to rise about five years before the report was published.[3]

The manipulation of the onset of the score decline was accompanied by other adjustments of reality. Take, for example, the prevailing interpretation. An acute decline began in the late sixties. Thus it can be traced, according to this view, to social turbulence caused by the civil-rights and other movements of the time. This version was accompanied by a remedy: a return to basics, understood to mean tougher discipline as well as a reduced curriculum—not to be applied across the board, but selectively, along class and racial lines.

Dissenters from this version offered extensive evidence for a different picture: Most test scores remained stable in the sixties; some even went up. The general decline was less acute than claimed. Moreover, it did not begin until the seventies, which makes it impossible to blame it on the social movements of the preceding decade. What caused it? Well, researchers who study long-term test-score trends believe a major factor was a maturity differential that affects test-taking skills, i.e., children were then entering school at a relatively younger age and were younger at each grade level.[4]

The manipulation of the test-score decline is consistent with the fact that the tests themselves are products of manipulation, whose use provides reliable information on sociopolitical trends, not on the status of the schools or the abilities of the students.

Score Watching

Not only is the public expected to follow scores with the avidity of investors following stocks, but it is also expected to believe that the slightest fluctuation has profound implications.

"The gain in SAT scores reflects the movement toward excellence in our schools that is sweeping the nation," proclaimed Secretary Bell a year after *A Nation at Risk* was published.[5] SAT math scores had risen 3 points on a 600-point scale; verbal scores had gone up 1 point.[6]

That there is no correlation between SAT scores and the status of education, except possibly an inverse one, is illustrated by the following: SAT scores began to decline in the sixties, creating a furor. Like the rise, the decline was (according to a prominent analyst of the SAT) grossly exaggerated.[7] One factor to which the decline was ascribed—and the one that accounted for the furor—was a "population change." In the sixties, blacks and other minorities began to take the SAT in substantially larger numbers, as did lower-income whites. The uproar over the score decline on a race- and class-biased test obscured the reality that the elite status of higher education had been significantly breached, and the level of education for the population as a whole was rising.

In the mid-seventies, the proportion of African-American high-school graduates entering colleges reached its peak. After 1976, the proportion declined, as it did for Latinos. In 1988 the decline continued, the American Council on Education reported in late 1989. In early 1990, the U.S. Department of Education announced, in an apparently contradictory report, that minority enrollment for 1986–1988 was at an all-time high. Many hailed the figures as the reversal of a trend, but the decline had not been halted. Because the nation's minority population had grown rapidly, the *number* of minority students entering colleges had risen, while the *proportion* of minority high-school graduates going on to higher education had declined.[8]

Those who interpreted the Department of Education figures as the reversal of a trend overlooked that the barriers to minority enrollment remain in place. Take, again, the SAT. In addition to screening out African-Americans and Latinos at the point of entry to college, it acts in very special ways to sustain the belief that these groups do not have academic ability. For example, in the late 1980s the media devoted intensive coverage to the controversy around athletic scholarships for youths with lower SAT scores. The coverage featured denunciations by test supporters of the treatment of this relatively small group, for whom the scholarships were the only route to college, as "pampering" and "special privileges." Although the youths were white as well as black, the influence of the old notion that blacks have athletic, not scholastic, aptitude was not difficult to detect.

Interestingly, test supporters did not direct accusations of pampering and special privileges at the large numbers of students who use expensive computerized courses, books, and coaching schools to raise their SAT scores. The head of one such school observed, "Most of our kids are wealthy. Those are the kids who have an advantage to begin with. And we're moving them up another level."[9] This school claims to raise SAT scores an average of 186 points. Since new coaching schools opened and others expanded in the eighties, their beat-the-test methods may be as good an explanation as any for the slight rise in SAT scores.

In any event, the decade closed with a significant confirmation that the SAT is not a measure of scholastic potential but a biased device. In 1989, Federal District Judge John M. Walker (New York) found that the SAT, as a means for awarding scholarships, discriminates against girls.[10]

II

A Nation at Risk is subtitled *The Imperative for Educational Reform*. Just what the report was intended to reform is not immediately apparent, given its silence on such matters as the funding gap between schools in affluent and poor areas, discrimination of any kind, segregation, and the inequities of the track system.

But the report does have its own notion of reform, according to which the schools can achieve "excellence" by raising "standards." Despite the impression this created, higher standards do not mean better standards, let alone better education. On the contrary, by demanding higher standards for students irrespective of their class and race, while remaining silent on class and racial discrimination, the report has helped to raise the barriers to education for students of lower socioeconomic and/or minority status.

That higher standards do not necessarily mean better standards is evident from the standards the report urged the schools to adopt: "Standardized tests of achievement . . . should be administered at major transition points from one level of schooling to another and particularly from high school to college or work. . . . The tests should be administered as part of a nationwide . . . system of State and local standardized tests."[11]

What *A Nation at Risk* called for is "minimum-competency" testing (MCT). At the time the report was published, thirty-six states had already begun MCT; most of the others soon followed suit. By the late seventies, MCT had become a hot issue in state election campaigns, whose buzzwords included "standards" and "excellence." Because the word "equity" was conspicuously missing, the impression was created that equality and excellence are mutually exclusive.

As soon as MCT was introduced, elected officials began to use the results to compare schools, compare groups of students, judge teachers, and allot or withhold funds.

"Florida Flunks"

Although not previously noted for leadership in education, the southern states were among the first to legislate competency testing. Florida, for instance, mandated the tests for grades 3 and 5 in 1976, and in 1977 began to give them also to eighth-grade and eleventh-year students. State officials lost no time in declaring themselves well satisfied in particular with the results for the high-school students.

"[I]f the Florida test were offered to others in other states, the scores would be similar. We took the leadership and found it out first," declared the state commissioner of education.[12] If the state's objective had in fact been to find out how students would perform on the tests, there would have been no point in giving them.

The schools, which had been officially segregated until 1967, were marked by de facto segregation and sharp socioeconomic distinctions. As if that were not basis enough for predicting the outcome, the state also conducted pre-tests that showed the failure rate would be between 25 and 30 percent, that African-American students would fall in disproportionate numbers below the arbitrary cutoff point, and that white students of lower socioeconomic status would also be adversely affected.[13] As it turned out, the predictions were on the conservative side. Nonetheless, the legislature hurriedly mandated that students must pass the state's competency test to get a high-school diploma, and that those who failed would be awarded a "certificate of attendance."

While Florida officials gave themselves high marks for competency, *Time* magazine reported that "Florida Flunks."[14] Others agreed. Black parents asserted that the state had been unconcerned with "protecting standards" while the schools were officially segregated, and that the tests would lead to resegregation through tracking.[15] Educators throughout the country were also disturbed. "Florida represents an educational system in the throes of disruption and dislocation," declared one, who added, "I doubt that the measurement experts will be around in Florida when the lawsuits are filed."[16]

"Fair Test" Ruling

The first lawsuit on minimum-competency tests was soon filed (*Debra P. v. Turlington*). The plaintiffs were black and white students who had been denied diplomas; the defendant was Florida's commissioner of education. In 1981, a federal appeals court handed down a decision that set a nationwide precedent for competency tests. It ruled that a state may not deprive students of the "economic and educational benefits of a diploma" unless it shows that its test is a "fair test" of what was taught in the classroom, and that the test's "racially discriminatory impact" is not due to "educational deprivation."[17]

Had the court strictly construed its own ruling, *all* states would have had to dismantle their MCT programs. Because educational deprivation did not end with official segregation, but continues through de facto segregation and resegregation through tracking, no state could show that a competency test's racially discriminatory effect is not attributable to this factor. Nor, given the disparities in education along class lines, could any state show that a competency test is a fair test of what was taught to children of lower socioeconomic status.

But the ruling was not intended to curtail MCT. This was made particularly evident by the fact that the court declared a moratorium on the tests, which supposedly allowed the state time to comply with the fair-test requirement. The moratorium also implied that the competency test's racially discriminatory effect was a vestige of past segregation. In other words, the fair-test ruling assumed that Florida had simply used the tests improperly and, given time, could use them properly. But there is no proper way to use a test that is intrinsically unfair.

"Who can successfully define the limits of competence and presume to measure accurately the 'competency' of test-takers?" asked the lawyer for the plaintiffs, who is also an educator.[18] The reason it is impossible to measure the competency of test takers is that "competency," like "intelligence," is an abstraction and so nonmeasurable. The psychometricians try to get around this insoluble problem in their usual way, i.e., by arbitrarily defining competency.

The tests used by the states as high-school diploma requirements are constructed on the assumption that competency can be measured by items calling for scholastic skills or, more often, by items that call for application of these skills to "adult-world" situations. Tests are also constructed to bring about a predetermined failure rate.[19]

Students who fail the test are labeled "functionally illiterate." The label implies they cannot read, but their failure is usually due to the math subtest. (Many adults who consider themselves quite literate may wonder how they would be classified if math were the criterion.) Nor does failure on this subtest necessarily mean a student does not have math skills. It may mean that the test requires the student to apply her or his skills in an unfamiliar and therefore culturally biased context—as, for example, when students from poor families are expected to balance a checkbook or handle a federal income-tax form. In many cases, students who fail the simulated adult-world tests go on to perform analogous tasks in real-life situations.

Nor does failure on a reading subtest mean a student cannot read. The International Reading Association concluded more than a decade ago that one can learn the "reading subskills" the tests call for without learning to read well, and vice versa.[20] The tests also include questions that overtly measure cultural values. One of these, the "good citizenship" subtest, offers a particularly instructive model of the trait it allegedly measures. By mandating social and personal behavior, it illegally infringes on an individual's freedom of choice.

Competency testing was imposed on the schools as an alleged assurance that children would learn the basics; instead it has profoundly distorted this process. A specialist in education observed: "By mandating educational outcomes through standardized tests . . . states set in motion a chain of events that alter educational ends and means. In effect, mandates say . . . don't teach children to read, just teach reading skills; don't teach children to write, just teach them to fill in the blanks."[21]

A Doctor's Discovery

In the late eighties John J. Cannell, a West Virginia doctor, learned that test scores in his state were above the national average. Since the public had been assured that the test-score rise that began in the late seventies was due to an insistence on "excellence" and "standards," he should have been delighted. But West Virginia has one of the highest nonliteracy rates in the country, and instead the doctor got angry. He also formed an organization, Friends for Education, that canvassed state education departments throughout the country. The group could not find a single state with scores below the national average.[22] (This statistical absurdity recalls the WWI tests, according to which the draftees had an average mental age of thirteen.)

The mystery of the rising scores on one hand, and the declining schools on the other, was not hard to solve. With the advent of minimum-competency tests, the practice of teaching to the test was converted into a more sophisticated one: Measurement Driven Instruction. With MDI, curriculums, teaching methods, and textbooks are aligned with preselected tests. The reason no state scored below average in the late eighties was that the tests had been standardized at the beginning of the decade, or before mere teaching to the test had been transformed into MDI.

At the same time that MDI demands conformity, it also reinforces inequality. In schools in poor areas, children are far less likely to be supplied with the textbooks and other materials designed to coordinate with the tests. But while these children in particular suffer from MDI, this approach—which encourages rote methods and student passivity—restricts and distorts education for all children subjected to it.

Testing the Teachers

The speed with which states mandated minimum-competency tests for students was equaled if not exceeded by the speed with which they mandated them for teachers. The states, observed a Rand Corporation social scientist, were in "a race to create a political symbol."[23] On an explicit level, the hastily created symbol stood for the pursuit of excellence; implicitly, it was emblematic of the presumed conflict between excellence and equity.

In 1978, only two states, South Carolina and Georgia, required minimum-competency tests for teachers. By 1986, forty-six states had adopted such programs (and three more were planning them). While all these states required the tests for certifying new teachers, some southern states also mandated them for practicing teachers. In addition, some states mandated competency tests for candidates for teacher-training programs.

The tests had immediate impact. In 1980, minority teachers made up 12.5 percent of the national teaching force, with African-Americans accounting for 8.6 percent. One year later, the proportion of black teachers had declined to 7.8 percent. In 1987, it was predicted that the minority teaching force could be reduced to 5 percent or less by the year 2000.[24] Not even a pragmatic consideration of severe proportions—a projected shortage of over one million teachers by the early nineties—braked an operation that was screening out minorities.

Thirty of the states that give competency tests use an ETS product, the NTE (National Teacher Examination). "Why do some people who do poorly on the NTE turn out to be, in the judgment of supervisors, good or excellent teachers? Why do some people who score quite well on the NTE turn out to be ineffective teachers?" asked a prominent educator in South Carolina, the first state to use the NTE.[25]

The answers are suggested both by what ETS did and did not claim for the NTE. ETS did not even attempt to claim that the test measured any of the personal characteristics a good teacher must have. What ETS did claim was that the NTE "reflects what appears to be a consensus among educators as to the knowledge important for a beginning teacher."[26] But no such consensus has ever existed.

The NTE has been the subject of a number of analyses, which revealed the following: the NTE is ambiguous; 40 percent of the questions in its "professional knowledge" section have no "right" answers. The NTE uses a simplistic multiple-choice format, whereas real-life problems in the classroom call for complex solutions. The "right" answers in the NTE's "general knowledge" section are biased in favor of middle- and upper-middle-class whites. The general knowledge section is also biased; more than twice as many women fail it as men, giving the latter an edge in a predominantly female profession.[27]

The NTE suffered a particularly acute blow when, in 1985, a federal district judge in Texas found intent to discriminate against African-Americans and Latinos in the state's use of an NTE derivative, the Pre-Professional Skills Test, as an admission requirement for teacher-training programs.

In 1988, ETS—without acknowledging the mounting opposition to the NTE—announced that this test would be replaced with a new one in 1992. According to ETS, the test, which will make use of computer simulations and other new techniques, is a "whole new approach to teacher certification."[28] But this is hardly the case. Not only will a test of "professional knowledge" be given in the old multiple-choice format, but the new techniques can offer a more sophisticated way for programming the old biases.

ETS is making every effort to win acceptance for the new test on the basis of advance claims. ETS should, however, be accorded the same treatment given any other organization introducing a new product: its claims should be weighed against its record. Moreover, unlike manufacturers who recall products known to be dangerously defective, ETS did not recall the NTE. The NTE will, it seems, be in use until the new test is ready. If ETS expected its new test to have a basically different result along racial, gender, and class lines, it is hard to believe it would have sanctioned continued use of the NTE.

But the new test aside, ETS' abandonment of the NTE has great significance. By its planned scrapping of a test that has served as a national measure of teacher competency, ETS itself calls into question the whole range of tests of student competency, ability, intelligence, aptitude, etc.

III

In contrast to *A Nation at Risk*, which takes standardized tests as its measure of excellence, *Barriers to Excellence: Our Children at Risk* makes major criticisms of testing.

The report was published by the National Coalition of Advocates for Students, a network of child-advocate groups that work on public school issues at federal, state, and local levels. In its opening paragraph, the report states, "While this report gives particular attention to those children who have shared least in the material benefits and economic opportunities of our society, it is ultimately a statement about *all* children and youth and about our society as a whole."[29]

The report is based on the findings of a citizens' Board of Inquiry, whose co-chairs were Marian Wright Edelman, president of the Children's Defense Fund, and Harold Howe II, formerly U.S. Commissioner of Education. The board held hearings in cities across the country, where teachers, parents, students, administrators, academics, elected and appointed officials, clergy, and representatives of civil-rights, labor, and other organizations testified that children are at risk from schools that practice class, racial, gender, and cultural discrimination. The groundbreaking project received financial support from many sources, including the Carnegie Corporation of New York, the Ford Foundation, the New World Foundation, and the Southern Education Foundation.

The Board of Inquiry—taking issue with the view that swept competency testing through state legislatures—stressed that "excellence without equity is both impractical and imcompatible with the goals of a democratic society."[30] The board heard expert testimony that competency testing has "dangerous" features, and that it places the greatest burden on the students who are most poorly served by the schools.[31] The board established testing's role in resegregating schools, i.e., it found a relationship between testing and the "[o]fficial policies and practices that . . . have undermined 30 years of efforts on behalf of desegregation."[32] The board condemned the use of IQ and other ability tests in labeling black children mentally retarded and for classifying children learning disabled.

At the same time that the Board of Inquiry's hearings demonstrated that minority and poor children suffer the most from the tests, they also showed that testing is harmful to *all* children. For example, the hearings revealed that elected officials and school administrators use the tests to compare schools, districts, and teachers in ways that are "often misleading."[33] With the growing political importance of the tests, the schools' agendas are increasingly related to "management and correlation to the testing program" rather than to mastery of the subjects. The tests, both teachers and parents testified, have become the "real curriculum."[34]

Barriers to Excellence also quotes a Boston teacher, whose remarks capture the day-to-day effect of standardized tests on both students and teachers:

> I like to figure out what is going on with a kid . . . but I'm bound in terms of certain objectives that the kids have to meet . . . . These objectives are judged by the school committee and by tests. Right now I'm really putting up a fight against these standardized tests . . . . I dislike that type of regimented testing. I think it's very cruel.[35]

IV

As the school year of 1989–90 got under way, education was in the news. In late September 1989, the president and governors held an "education summit" that called for a "major restructuring" of the educational system. The phrasing was undeniably militant. Yet nothing that came out of that meeting offered the slightest promise of a substantively different direction for the schools. Where the previous call for reform, *A Nation at Risk*, had been silent, the new one was too, standing mute on such matters as tracking, segregation, and the funding gap between schools for the affluent and those for the poor. Nor did the call project a break with the standardized tests advocated by its predecessor; on the contrary, it suggested there would be more of the same. In fact, it endorsed "school choice," which imperils public education by putting schools on a "free-market" basis.[36]

But education was also in the news for another reason: a book about a teacher and her students, *Among Schoolchildren*, was on the nonfiction best-seller lists.[37] Significantly, the setting for the book is not an atypical or "model" school, but one where the conditions replicate those the Board of Inquiry found in schools throughout the country.

Among Schoolchildren is also significant for another reason. In the early years of the decade, teachers were the objects of negative campaigning by certain powerful forces—as is evident, for example, in *A Nation at Risk*.[38] Now it seemed that *Among Schoolchildren*—which portrays a teacher as dedicated and caring, not to mention "feisty, funny, and tough"[39]—might be both a harbinger and shaper of a different view of teachers. But if old attitudes are to be replaced, the change will not come about in isolation but in the context of other changes. And change is not what the author, Tracy Kidder, had in mind. In an interview, he expressed a view that he also projected, albeit more subtly, in his book. "We like to generalize about education, and look for grand solutions, often forgetting that there's something very compelling about what goes on in a classroom. It's a small world where 'small things' loom large."[40]

Just why there should be a conflict between recognizing the small world of the classroom as compelling and looking for solutions is difficult to grasp. Actually, what goes on in the classrooms is best taken as an impetus for seeking solutions. But not "grand solutions." "Grand solutions" sounds perilously close to "grand illusions."

Kelly School, where *Among Schoolchildren* takes place, is in Holyoke, a small industrial city in Massachusetts. The school's population mirrors that of the city; of its 620 students, 30 are African-American, 265 white, and 314 Latino, mainly Puerto Rican. About 60 percent of the children come from families receiving public assistance. Two-thirds of the class that Kidder spent a year with filled out forms for free lunches.

True to his philosophy, Kidder works on a small scale, portraying the class through a series of closeups—compelling shots of "ordinary" interactions between the teacher, Chris Zajac, and her students. Yet Kidder sees the classroom as not only a small world but an insular one; he describes Zajac's classroom as a "sealed-off domain."[41] Still, the relationships in the classroom are so absorbing one may easily forget what is missing from the picture. A reviewer filled in the blanks. "We know little or nothing about the faculty at Kelly School. We don't learn about any saints or scoundrels in the superintendent's office because we never get there. As for public education policy makers in Massachusetts or elsewhere, they're essentially out of the book."[42]

Of course, it is impossible to record events in a classroom without suggesting the influence of the world beyond. Kidder's description of the start of a school day is evidence enough of this point:

> At eight, a high-pitched beep from the intercom announced math, which lasted an hour. Some children left [Zajac's] room for math, replaced by some children from the room next door. For math and reading, children . . . were grouped by abilities. Her lower math group began the year with a review of the times tables and her top group with decimals . . . . [E]very member of the low group had to master long division at least, and all of the top group should get at least to the brink of geometry.[43]

Only eight fifth-graders are on the high math track. They come from two different homerooms. Zajac has twenty children in hers. So it seems that about four-fifths of the children are classified "slow learners." Obviously, children on the crowded low track will get much less attention than those on the spacious high one. Each year the gap will widen between what the children on the high and low tracks learn. And the children on the low math track are in almost all cases on lower reading tracks too.

The track system has left its telltale mark. "I'm stupid. I'm stupid in every subject," exclaims a crying Felipe, unconvinced by his teacher's efforts to assure him he is bright.[44] And when the teacher asks Jimmy, a white boy from a poor neighborhood, why he does not like to be called on in math, he answers, "Because. It makes me feel stupid."[45]

There is no hint of the testing controversy in *Among School-children*. But this should not be taken to mean there is a lack of testing at Kelly School. Although the children are described as being grouped by "abilities," we can be sure they have instead been grouped by ability tests. The California Achievement Test is administered (offstage) by Zajac to the class. The school also gives "core examinations"—which feature a battery of IQ and other tests—to children assumed to be slow learners, emotionally disturbed, troublemakers, etc. One recipient of a "core" is Clarence, who is described as a "small, lithe, brown-skinned boy."[46] After his problem has been "diagnosed," he is exiled to a special school, where the children sit at desks with high partitions on three sides.

Any possible notion of the class as a sealed-off entity is shattered when the local paper publishes the results of a state-wide competency test for third-, sixth-, and ninth-graders. Holyoke children get some of the worst scores in the state. More than 30 percent of the Kelly sixth-graders fail. Almost all the children who flunk come from poor and minority families.

"I don't want to hear the test scores anymore," exclaims the principal. "I know what kids we got here. We can't bring them all up to grade level no matter what we do."[47] Clearly, the principal has absorbed the message of one or another influential document—perhaps the Coleman Report, with its thesis that educational outcomes are determined by the children's family environment, rendering the quality of schooling quite irrelevant. Indeed, in one way and another, *Among Schoolchildren* tells us repeatedly that the onus for the scholastic failure of poor children falls on the children and their families.

Among Schoolchildren informs its readers of strong anti–Puerto Rican bias among some Kelly teachers. But no suggestion is made of a connection between anti–Puerto Rican or anti–African-American bias—whether in tests, texts, administrators, or teachers—and the teaching-learning process. Except, in a fleeting scene, by Clarence.

A student teacher orders Clarence to stand in the hall. From there he watches as she orders a white boy, whom she has also accused of misbehavior, to go to the principal's office. The boy refuses, and the teacher allows him to stay. Offering a diagnosis overlooked by the core examination, Clarence exclaims, "She prejudice, too. See, she didn't get Robert."[48]

The Pyramid

That underestimating the teacher's responsibility does teachers and education a grave disservice is obvious. But what may be less obvious is that overestimating it does the same. By portraying the teacher as the center of a small world, Kidder seemed to give recognition to the teacher's importance. In reality, however, he placed teachers in a false, untenable position.

> Most teachers have little control over school policy or curriculum or choice of texts or special placement of students, but most have a great deal of autonomy inside their classrooms. To a degree shared by only a few other occupations . . . , public education rests precariously on the skill and virtue of the people at the bottom of the institutional pyramid. Chris had nearly absolute autonomy inside her room.[49]

This is a quite startling interpretation. If teachers have little control over (and little input to) policy, curriculum, etc., how can they have autonomy? It might also be argued that autonomy is an illusory issue, and the real one is how to achieve a situation where teachers can function more productively.

What a teacher does in the classroom is circumscribed by school policies and practices, which the teacher may accept quietly or do battle with (at her or his own peril). When this fact is overlooked, and it is claimed that education rests on the "skill and virtue"—words that take on different meanings for different people—of those at the bottom of the pyramid, teachers can be held responsible for the crisis in the schools, just as they were when under attack in the early eighties.

Chris Zajac does her impressive best to achieve the goals set by the school system. Her concern for her students stays with her after she leaves the classroom, haunting her even in recurring dreams. By her own estimate, she is able to make a difference for individual children, not for the class as a whole. But the responsibility for such an outcome should not be placed on her. Kelly School's mode of operation, including the kind of teacher-expectations that it encourages, determines the results it gets. Two researchers have described the scene at the nation's Kelly schools:

> The [children of the poor] are catalogued, measured and deemed wanting the moment they enter school; they are tested before they are instructed. The teacher becomes a judge; the class' standing in reading and arithmetic is a yardstick of collective failure; and the fear of inadequacy pervades the classroom, suffocating teacher and pupil alike.[50]

At Kelly School there may well be faculty members who question the cataloguing and measuring. But in *Among Schoolchildren*, we never met them. Because *Among Schoolchildren* made no distinction between the way things are and the way they should and could be, Kelly School's mode of operation assumed the status of an immutable order.

In *Barriers to Excellence: Our Children at Risk*, the same scene is surveyed: the report tells of Kelly schools and worse. But where *Among Schoolchildren* treats the prevailing, Kelly-type schooling as appropriate, *Barriers to Excellence* offers compelling evidence against it. Through the witness of teachers, administrators and others, it testifies to the need for the schools to move away from the cataloguing and measuring—the yardsticks of failure—that put millions of children at risk.

One Man's Dream, Another's Nightmare

I

A baby sits, pen in hand, at a desk. He is looking at something spread out on the desk. It is an intelligence test. Above him are the words, "The Next Generation of Intelligence Tests." The baby, who appears on a 1979 cover of *Psychology Today*, seems to be in the pink of health. "Pink" is used advisedly; it tinges his white skin, signifying the medical and nutritional advantages available to children of a certain class and race. "His" is also used advisedly; the baby appears to be male. In short, the child model correlates perfectly with the testers' model of a model child.

Inside the magazine, articles tell of the next-generation tests. One is for infants (ages three months to three years). In taking this test, a child is exposed to visual episodes typified by the following: a small car rolls down a ramp, knocks over a doll, is picked up by a hand, and is then rolled back up the ramp. The episode is repeated six times. The next time, the doll is hit but does not fall. The heartbeat of the child watching this little horror-movie scenario is monitored via electrocardiogram leads attached to her/his chest, while unseen observers record the child's facial expressions. The speed with which the child reacts to the altered sequence is taken as the measure of the child's intelligence.[1] The expense of administering this test probably assures that most babies will not be subjected to it.

This test was not the first one for infants. A "standard" IQ test for this age group, which tests neuromotor skills (such as those used in stacking blocks), had already been in use for some time. From the psychometricians' standpoint, the problem with the test is that its results do not correlate with school- or preschool-age IQ tests.

In 1989, there came the announcement that a new test had produced the desired correlations. With this test, babies six months to one year old are shown pictures. It is assumed they will be more interested in new than familiar stimuli, and so will spend more time looking at new pictures than ones they have seen before. (Never mind that some people prefer familiar things.) The length of time the baby spends looking at a new picture is assumed to be a test of the baby's visual memory, which is in turn assumed to be a measure of the baby's intelligence.

The vaunted correlations were attained in the following way. The test was given to fifty-five babies from upper-middle-class families. After three years they were retested on a picture-vocabulary test. A high percentage of those who scored above average on the infant test also scored above average on the second test. Although correlations between the two tests may well prove something, it is hardly their validity. What the correlations point to—given that different attitudes are routinely conveyed to children who score above average and those who do not, and that there were three years in which to convey them—is the effect of adult expectations on a child's performance.

The test has been placed on the market. It has not been advertised as a test for upper-middle-class babies but rather for poor ones, i.e., as a test that will predict below-average intelligence in poor children, who can then, according to the psychologist who devised it, be given an "enriched" education. Other psychologists have, however, criticized the test as one that will label infants.[2]

The possibility that this or some other infant intelligence test could become widely used hardly seems remote if one is aware that tests are now being given to decide whether children are "ready" for kindergarten. Although children mature at different rates and learn different things in different class and cultural settings, these tests arbitrarily designate certain tasks as a measure of "developmental" age, as compared to "chronological" age. The original rationale for these tests was that they would identify children with special needs. But in reality, children who did not do well on these IQ-test spinoffs were stigmatized as mentally underdeveloped. Thus the tests' newer use as pass-fail exams is not a "misuse," but an extension of their original use.

"Readiness" tests are also being used to decide whether kindergarteners should be promoted to first grade. Research shows that the children held in kindergarten for an extra year, or kept from entering it for an extra year, do no better than those who stay with their age group. Holding children back, however, vastly increases the risk that they will not finish high school.[3] The grave effects of holding children back are also evident from a study of failed kindergarteners, who rated the experience as just slightly less stressful than losing a parent or going blind.[4]

Many relatively affluent parents are treating the kindergarten and first-grade entrance exams as junior SAT's. They are having their children tutored or coaching the children themselves with the help of such manuals as *The Baby Boards: A Parents' Guide to Preschool and Primary School Entrance Tests.*[5]

The Rivals

Another article in the same issue of *Psychology Today* tells of a new concept of intelligence. It is a variant of the "information processing" thesis, a theory of intelligence inspired by computer models of cognitive operations. The psychometrician who created the new concept envisions a hierarchic mental structure in which "meta-components" preside over lower-level components (or, as he would later describe it, where "executive" intelligence presides over "worker" components).[6]

A test allegedly based on this concept (or, to be exact, on an elaborated version of it) is being made available to the schools by the Psychological Corporation, a major test maker. According to the psychometrician who created the test as well as the concept, the test measures the abilities needed for real-world professional and personal success. Ironically, while he claims his test measures the abilities needed for nonacademic success, his chosen measure is the same one used in IQ tests: academic skills. Like its ancestor, the next-generation test is composed of analogies, vocabulary questions, number-based questions, etc.[7] As a test demanding skills that are differentially available along class and racial lines, it can be depended upon to sort test takers in the usual way.

A criticism often made of IQ tests is that they were constructed without a guiding theory. Because he first devised a theory and then a test, the psychometrician maintains he has overcome this criticism. He could, however, just as easily have reversed the order; just as his new test is a variant of IQ tests, his new concept is a variant of concepts that came in the wake of IQ tests. For example, he maintains that the component, which is the basic unit in the mental structure he envisions, is a "definable entity."[8] There is no reason to argue over whether the component is definable; the point is whether it is discernible. As it turns out, evidence of its existence is as elusive as proof of Spearman's g or Thurstone's PMA's, which exist only as inferences from correlations among tests based on shared assumptions. In other words, a contemporary psychometrician has followed the examples set by two early ones by inventing a model of cognitive functioning and treating its presumed components as though their existence had already been demonstrated.

As was the case with Spearman and Thurstone, the creator of the new test has a rival. The rival asserts that "we should get away altogether from tests and correlations among tests."[9] So far, so good. But rivals often make accurate criticisms of their adversaries, only to express fallacies of their own. In this case, the rival has his own concept of intelligence, according to which there are seven separate, biologically based "intelligences" (logical-mathematical, linguistic, spatial, musical, bodily-kinesthetic, interpersonal, and intrapersonal).[10] At least this is what he originally claimed; at last count, he had raised the number to twenty.[11]

The rival psychologist says he does not like tests. He does, however, want to measure intelligence. Thus he proposes a supposedly new method that actually reverts to the *overtly* subjective assessments made before the IQ method introduced *covert* subjectivity. In his method, "assessment specialists" in the schools would determine which type of intelligence a child has by observing the child's selection and use of games, puzzles, etc.; after the first few grades, the school would use the child's "cognitive profile" to match the child with curriculum and future work.[12]

That there is no reason to believe such assessments would diverge in essence from the standardized ones is evident, for example, from the following. Although the rival psychologist claimed to oppose tests, he introduced his method of measuring intelligence under the aegis of ETS; he also maintained that IQ tests measure the type of intelligence needed for academic success.[13] And the psychologist who created the next-generation test also held that IQ tests play this role.[14]

In the mid-eighties, a *New York Times* writer reviewed the supposedly new methods of measuring intelligence and then commented:

> To be sure, the 200 or so intelligence measures currently available, and particularly the half-dozen most commonly used by schools, will not soon disappear from the scene . . . .
>
> I.Q. tests have an unquestioned utility in the eyes of many educators and psychologists . . . . [T]he tests can help educators place [a child] in a setting that best suits him.[15]

So, instead of allowing the new tests to displace IQ tests, the testers are using them to further entrench IQ tests as the classic instrument for measuring academic abilities.

Binet's Dream, Lippmann's Nightmare

The argument that IQ tests in particular and abilities tests in general help the schools place children in suitable settings is based on two assumptions. One is evident: that the tests assess individual differences. The other is that assessment should precede education.

The significance of the second assumption becomes apparent when one recognizes that the tests are not instruments for assessing individual differences, but a means for ignoring individuality and slotting children according to prior assumptions about the races and classes they belong to. By using the tests to assess the children—i.e., to decide whether or not a child should be given a high-quality academic education—the schools can continue, ad infinitum, to justify superior and inferior education along class and racial lines.

Only when the schools pass judgment on the tests, instead of using the tests to pass judgment on the children, can a process leading to individual assessment begin. To advance the process, the schools would also have to reverse their priorities so that education, not assessment, becomes the primary objective, and at the same time strive to overcome racial, class, and sex discrimination. When the schools encourage all children to aspire, provide them with equal opportunities to learn, and a curriculum that includes the contributions of the cultures and the gender whose true roles have historically been omitted, it will become possible, as the children mature, to assess their individual abilities and inclinations.

The rush to pass judgment on the children has brought far more than the realization of Binet's dream of an ideal city where everyone would be tested; it has created an entire society where the citizens are tested over and over again.

It has been a long time since Lippmann warned that it would be "a thousand times better" if "all the intelligence testers and all their questionnaires" were "sunk without warning in the Sargasso Sea" than to let the impression take root that intelligence tests "really measure intelligence." Often it is too late to act on a warning that has long gone unheeded—especially when the danger has already come to pass. Yet even an impression that has taken root can be uprooted.

Suppose the stern but just measures Lippmann called for were carried out. Or suppose, instead, that in a spirit of humaneness the testers have never shown, their fate were reconsidered, and they—but not their tests—were spared. Spared, but not pardoned.

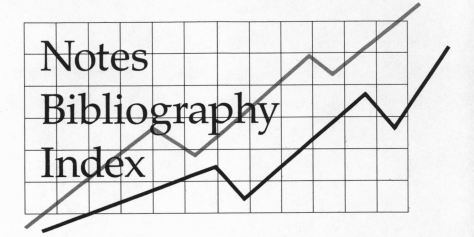

Notes
Bibliography
Index

Notes

Introduction

1. Harold Brodkey, *Stories in an Almost Classical Mode* (New York: Knopf, 1988), 221.
2. Ibid., 291.
3. The classic study was Robert Rosenthal and Lenore Jacobson, *Pygmalion in the Classroom: Teacher Expectation and Pupils' Intellectual Development* (New York: Holt, Rinehart and Winston, 1968).
4. Leon Botstein, ". . . Then Why Do They Offer Band-Aids and Gimmicks?" *New York Times*, August 17, 1988, A23.
5. Fred Hechinger, "About Education," *New York Times*, December 7, 1988, B17.
6. Alec M. Gallup and Stanley M. Elam, "Twentieth Annual Gallup Poll of the Public's Attitude Toward the Public Schools," *Phi Delta Kappan* 70 (September 1988): 41.
7. Ibid.
8. George F. Madeus, director of the Center for the Study of Testing, Evaluation, and Educational Policy, Boston College. Quoted by Edward B. Fiske, "U.S. Testing of Students Raises Growing Debate," *New York Times*, December 27, 1987, A1.
9. Larry Cuban, associate dean of education, Stanford University. Quoted by Edward B. Fiske, "National Testing: Many Questions," *New York Times*, December 30, 1987, B8.

1. IQ: Status of a Symbol

1. Andrew J. Strenio, Jr., *The Testing Trap* (New York: Rawson, Wade, 1981), 20.
2. Judge Robert F. Peckham, quoted in ibid., 68.
3. The study was conducted by the National Center for Fair and Open Testing (FairTest). See D. Monty Neill and Noe J. Medina, "Standardized Testing: Harmful to Educational Health," *Phi Delta Kappan* 70 (May 1989): 688–89.
4. Alexandra K. Wigdor and Wendell R. Garner, eds., *Ability Testing: Uses, Consequences, and Controversies,* Part 1 (Washington, D.C.: National Academy Press, 1982), iii. Immediately after *Ability Testing* was pub-

163

lished, it was praised by Gregory R. Anrig, president of ETS, but it came under fire from Allan Nairn, a consumer advocate, who said that it "toed the industry line in most cases" (quoted by Robert Reinhold, "Standardized Tests Defended by Panel," *New York Times,* February 3, 1982, A17). Two years before this, Nairn had prepared a report for the Ralph Nader organization denouncing the testing industry.

5. Wigdor and Garner, *Ability Testing,* 204.

6. Diane Ravitch, "Value of Standardized Tests in Indicating How Well Students Are Learning," in Charles W. Daves, ed., *The Uses and Misuses of Tests* (San Francisco: Jossey-Bass, 1984), 60.

7. Wigdor and Garner, *Ability Testing,* viii.

8. Ibid., 1.

9. Quoted by Strenio, *The Testing Trap,* 22.

10. Wigdor and Garner, *Ability Testing,* 113.

11. In 1980, in *PASE v. Hannon,* Federal District Judge John F. Grady upheld the use of IQ tests for assigning black children to EMR classes in the Chicago area.

12. Fred M. Hechinger, "About Education," *New York Times,* September 6, 1983, C7.

13. See Vincent P. Franklin, "Black Social Scientists and the Mental Testing Movement, 1920–1940," in Reginald L. Jones, ed., *Black Psychology,* 2d ed. (New York: Harper and Row, 1980), 205.

14. W.E.B. Du Bois, *Dusk of Dawn: An Essay Toward an Autobiography of a Race Concept* (New York: Shocken Books, 1971), 99–100. First published 1940.

15. Quoted by Samuel Bowles and Herbert Gintis, *Schooling in Capitalist America: Educational Reform and the Contradictions of Economic Life* (New York: Basic Books, 1976), 195.

16. Walter Lippmann, "The Mystery of the 'A' Men," in N.J. Block and Gerald Dworkin, eds., *The IQ Controversy: Critical Readings* (New York: Pantheon, 1976), 8–9.

17. Arthur R. Jensen, "How Much Can We Boost IQ and Scholastic Achievement?" *Harvard Educational Review* 39 (Winter 1969): 1–123.

18. Walter Lippmann, "The Abuse of the Tests," in Block and Dworkin, *The IQ Controversy,* 19.

19. The post-Lippmann environmentalists are discussed in Chapter 8.

20. Adrienne Harris, "Are Brains Genetic?" (review of *The Intelligence Controversy,* H.J. Eysenck vs. Leon Kamin), *New York Times Book Review,* May 3, 1981, 11.

2. IQ's Skeletons

1. Stephen Jay Gould, "Racist Arguments and IQ," in Ashley Montagu, ed., *Race and IQ* (New York: Oxford University Press, 1975), 146. First published in *Natural History*, May 1974.

2. For a discussion of craniometrics from a scientific and social standpoint, focusing in particular on phrenology, see Stephan L. Chorover, *From Genesis to Genocide: The Meaning of Human Nature and the Power of Behavior Control* (Cambridge: MIT Press, 1979), 142–48.

3. Ibid., 148.

4. R.C. Lewontin, "The Inferiority Complex" (review of *The Mismeasure of Man*, by Stephen Jay Gould), *New York Review of Books*, October 22, 1981, 16.

5. Ibid.

6. Stephen Jay Gould, *The Mismeasure of Man* (New York: Norton, 1981), 25.

7. Ibid., 150.

8. Ibid., 155.

9. Ibid., 153.

10. Ibid., 152.

11. Ibid.

12. Quoted in ibid., 152.

13. Quoted in ibid., 154.

14. Quoted in ibid., 150.

15. Ibid., 151.

16. Ibid., 148–49.

17. Quoted by Theta H. Wolf, *Alfred Binet* (Chicago: University of Chicago Press, 1973), 155.

18. Gould, *The Mismeasure of Man*, 149.

19. Ibid., 154.

20. Quoted in ibid., 154.

21. Ibid.

22. Alfred Binet and Théodore Simon, *The Development of Intelligence in Children (The Binet-Simon Scale)*, translated by Elizabeth S. Kite (Vineland, N.J.: Vineland Training School; Baltimore: Williams and Wilkins, 1916), 305.

23. Ibid., 262.

24. Quoted by Wolf, *Alfred Binet*, 188. Binet's reference to "criminal anthropology" reflects the influence on his thinking of biological deter-

minism. Criminal anthropology was the invention of Cesare Lombroso, who attempted to establish stigmata—such as darker skin, larger jaws, and low and narrow foreheads—for identifying "born criminals."

3. IQ Takes Over

1. Lewis M. Terman, *The Measurement of Intelligence: An Explanation of and a Complete Guide for the Use of the Stanford Revision and Extension of the Binet-Simon Intelligence Scale* (Boston: Houghton Mifflin, 1916), 115.

2. Ibid., 91–92.

3. Quoted by Allan Chase, *The Legacy of Malthus: The Social Costs of the New Scientific Racism* (New York: Knopf, 1977), 249.

4. Quoted in ibid.

5. Robert M. Yerkes, ed., "Psychological Examining in the United States Army," *Memoirs of the National Academy of Sciences,* vol. 15 (Washington, D.C.: U.S. Government Printing Office, 1921). Offering a rationale for the testers' segregation of blacks' scores from whites', which also served as a "scientific" justification for segregation in the army, Yerkes stated, "This procedure is partly a matter of convenience since the separation of the men in the Army most usually is reflected by a separation of the records in the files, but the striking differences in intelligence ratings that occur between negro and white groups also indicate that a combination of the two types would simply serve to obscure the fundamental and vital differences" (ibid., 559). "Psychological Examining in the United States Army" also provides revealing pictorial evidence of the context in which testing emerged; it includes a photo of blacks lined up in front of a barrack as they wait to be tested, as well as photos of blacks and whites being tested separately.

6. Chase, *Legacy of Malthus,* 253.

7. Carl C. Brigham, *A Study of American Intelligence* (Princeton, N.J.: Princeton University Press, 1923), 210.

8. Ibid., vii.

9. For specimens of this testimony, see Leon J. Kamin, *The Science and Politics of I.Q.* (Potomac, Md.: Lawrence Erlbaum, 1974), 23–26. The book provides an exposé of mental measurement's early years.

10. Almost sixty years after the Immigration Act was passed, Mark Snyderman and Richard J. Herrnstein assailed Kamin, Gould, and others for holding that the mental testers and the WWI data played an important role in bringing about its passage (Snyderman and Herrn-

stein, "Intelligence Tests and the Immigration Act of 1924," *American Psychologist* 38 [September 1983]: 986–95). They base their argument on the number of references to mental tests in the legislative record (which, by their own account, they did not review exhaustively). This reductionist approach simply ignores the extensive documentation by Kamin, Chase, Chorover, and others of the many-sided activities of the testing movement for over a decade in legitimating and inflaming the xenophobic and racist atmosphere in which the Immigration Act and the related eugenic-sterilization laws were passed.

Snyderman and Herrnstein also overlook the refutation of their argument that appeared in a definitive original source. In his foreword to Brigham's book, Yerkes declared that the author had performed a "notable service to psychology, to sociology, and *above all to our law makers*" with his "illuminating discussion [of] the data relative to intelligence and nativity," i.e., the WWI test statistics on foreign-born draftees (Brigham, *American Intelligence*, vi–vii; emphasis added).

11. Chorover, *From Genesis to Genocide*, 68.

12. Wigdor and Garner, *Ability Testing*, 89.

13. Ibid., 88.

14. Ibid.

15. Gould, *The Mismeasure of Man*, 201.

16. Ibid., 224.

17. Ibid., 198.

18. Ibid.

19. Ibid., 195.

20. Wolf, *Alfred Binet*, 309.

21. Gould, *The Mismeasure of Man*, 194–95.

22. Wigdor and Garner, *Ability Testing*, 88.

23. Quoted by Franklin, "Black Social Scientists and the Mental Testing Movement, 1920–1940," 207.

24. Otto Klineberg, *Negro Intelligence and Selective Migration* (New York: Columbia University Press, 1935), 2.

25. M.F. Ashley Montagu, "Intelligence of Northern Negroes and Southern Whites in the First World War," *American Journal of Psychology* 58 (April 1945): 161–88.

26. Ibid., 186.

27. Ibid.

28. Gould, *The Mismeasure of Man*, 232.

29. Ibid.

30. Ibid., 233.

31. Douglas Lee Eckberg, *Intelligence and Race: The Origins and Dimensions of the IQ Controversy* (New York: Praeger, 1979), 205n.

32. Carl C. Brigham, "Intelligence Tests of Immigrant Groups," *Psychological Review* 37 (March 1930): 158–65.

33. Ibid., 164.

34. Ibid., 165.

35. Ibid., 158.

4. The IQ Hierarchy

1. Wigdor and Garner, *Ability Testing*, 90.

2. "Meritocracy" was created by a British sociologist, Michael Young, for a satirical work, *The Rise of the Meritocracy, 1870–2033: An Essay on Education and Equality* (London: Thames and Hudson, 1958).

3. Eckberg, *Intelligence and Race*, 112.

4. James M. Lawler, *IQ, Heritability and Racism* (New York: International, 1978).

5. Ibid., 85.

6. Ibid., 23.

7. Ibid., 25.

8. Ibid., 27.

9. Ibid., 6.

10. Ibid., 39. The term "non-white," which appears in the quotation, has an affinity to the IQ method: it assumes a single, white norm and implicitly classifies those of other colors as deviations from the norm.

11. Ibid., 41.

12. Ibid., 42.

13. Quoted by Gould in *The Mismeasure of Man*, 149. (Gould describes this statement as Binet's "famous dictum.") When Binet says the "tests" should be "numerous," he is actually referring to the subtests, or groups of related items that make up a test. Subtests are still often referred to simply as "tests."

14. Chorover, *From Genesis to Genocide*, 37.

15. Lawler, *IQ, Heritability and Racism*, 42–43.

16. Ibid., 43.

17. Lawler's proposed test is discussed in Chapter 9.

18. Lawler, *IQ, Heritability and Racism*, 44.

19. Ibid., 47.

20. Ibid.

21. Ibid.

5. The Surrogate Stratagem

1. Lewis M. Terman, "The Great Conspiracy," in Block and Dworkin, *The IQ Controversy*, 33.

2. Banesh Hoffmann, *The Tyranny of Testing* (New York: Crowell-Collier, 1962), 214.

3. The *Oxford English Dictionary* devotes almost a page to showing that "intelligent" and "intelligence" have been used "continuously since the late fourteenth century to mean precisely what people commonly mean by these terms today," points out Chorover, *From Genesis to Genocide*, 52.

4. Quoted by R.J. Herrnstein, *I.Q. in the Meritocracy* (Boston: Atlantic Monthly Press, and Little, Brown, 1973), 107.

5. Chorover, *From Genesis to Genocide*, 52.

6. Lawler, *IQ, Heritability and Racism*, 33.

7. Wigdor and Garner, *Ability Testing*, 74.

8. In Chapter 6, we discuss why a test can be described as nonbiased in the statistical sense when it is biased in the usual sense.

9. Quoted by Paul L. Houts, "A Conversation with Banesh Hoffmann," in Paul L. Houts, ed., *The Myth of Measurability* (New York: Hart, 1977), 208.

10. Ibid.

11. Lawler, *IQ, Heritability and Racism*, 71.

12. Ibid., 25. Lawler's assertion is also accompanied by a justification: "Of course, the IQ test was not totally arbitrary, and reflected something in it. Any concept or abstraction from reality that arises in a practical situation usually contains some aspect of the reality it reflects." The contention that an abstraction from reality contains some aspect of the reality it reflects emerges, upon examination, as a tautology: an abstraction reflects what it reflects. Nor is there anything distinctive about an abstraction that arises in a practical or real situation; *all* concepts arise in this way. The point is that certain concepts arise as a reflection of reality and others—e.g., those that assume (as does the IQ concept) that a mental hierarchy underlies the social hierarchy—as a falsification of it.

13. Ibid., 84.

14. Gould, *The Mismeasure of Man*, 199.

15. Phyllis Rosser, *The SAT Gender Gap: Identifying the Causes* (Washington, D.C.: Center for Women Policy Studies, 1989), 3. This study is discussed in Chapter 6.

16. Buell G. Gallagher, ed. "Editor's Foreword," *NAACP Report on Minority Testing* (New York: NAACP Special Contribution Fund, 1976), i.

17. Terman, *The Measurement of Intelligence*, 315–17.

18. Ibid., 317. Terman also failed the answer "A divorce," which was "very common with the children tested . . . at Reno."

19. Amado M. Padilla and Blas M. Garza, "I.Q. Tests: A Case of Cultural Myopia," in Houts, *The Myth of Measurability*, 130–31.

20. "The Score Against IQ: A Look at Some Test Items," in Houts, *The Myth of Measurability*, 102.

21. Ibid., 104.

22. Ibid., 101.

23. Ibid., 100.

24. Judah L. Schwartz, "A is to B as C is to Anything at All: The Illogic of IQ Tests," in Houts, *The Myth of Measurability*, 95.

6. The Other Side of the Tracks

1. Wigdor and Garner, *Ability Testing*, 110.

2. Quoted by Clarence J. Karier, "Testing for Order and Control in the Corporate Liberal State," in Block and Dworkin, *The IQ Controversy*, 358.

3. Quoted in Ronald Smothers, "In Pupil 'Tracks,' Many See a Means of Resegregation," *New York Times*, February 18, 1990, p. E5.

4. Selma's student population was 70 percent African-American. Before Norward Roussell became superintendent, students were tracked according to the assessments of school personnel. All but 3 percent of the black students at Selma High School, whatever their test scores or school grades, were put on low tracks, while 90 percent of the white students were put on the high track. An additional 7 percent of blacks were placed on the high track after Roussell stipulated that tracking be governed either by scores or grades. But since the bias of the old way of tracking was replicated in the tests and in the schools, blacks *as a whole* (90 percent) stayed on the low tracks they had been consigned to when tracking was *openly* by race. (Figures appear in Smothers, "In Pupil 'Tracks,' Many See A Means of Resegregation.") Roussell also stipulated that students from lower tracks be permitted to enter aca-

demic classes, i.e., classes that would otherwise have been off-limits to most black students. However, students who enter such courses from lower tracks are still penalized by unequal academic preparation, and by the influence of tracking on teacher expectations.

Black parents in Selma organized BEST (Better Education Support Team), which has fought for equal educational opportunities and to renew Roussell's contract. To combat the effects of resegregation, BEST also holds Saturday classes, whose primary objective is to help children gain self-esteem. Rose Sanders, a Selma attorney and coordinator of BEST, provided information on the steps taken by Roussell and on BEST's activities (phone conversation, February 28, 1990).

5. Lawler, *IQ, Heritability and Racism,* 58.

6. Gould, *The Mismeasure of Man,* 155.

7. Richard H. de Lone, for the Carnegie Council on Children, *Small Futures: Children, Inequality and the Limits of Liberal Reform* (New York: Harcourt Brace Jovanovich, 1979), 71.

8. Ibid., 106.

9. Wigdor and Garner, *Ability Testing,* 112.

10. For example, in *PASE v. Hannon,* Judge Grady went through the IQ tests used to assign black children to EMR classes in the Chicago area. After deciding that only a few items might be biased, he ruled, "[T]hese few items do not render the tests unfair." Quoted by Nathan Glazer, "IQ on Trial," *Commentary* (June 1981), 58.

11. Wigdor and Garner, *Ability Testing,* 75.

12. Schwartz, "A Is to B as C Is to Anything at All," 92.

13. Wigdor and Garner, *Ability Testing,* 60.

14. Quoted by N.J. Block and Gerald Dworkin, "IQ, Heritability, and Inequality," in Block and Dworkin, *The IQ Controversy,* 463.

15. Lewontin, "The Inferiority Complex," 15.

16. Gould, *The Mismeasure of Man,* 251.

17. Ibid., 238.

18. Lewontin, "The Inferiority Complex," 16.

19. Gould, *The Mismeasure of Man,* 310. Curiously enough, despite his argument against *g,* Gould also leaves an opening for it: *g,* he states, is "neither clearly a thing, nor necessarily innate if a thing" (ibid., 320). In other words, *g* may or may not be what Spearman claimed it to be. Lewontin, by contrast, is not an agnostic: after showing that the different test parts correlate with each other because they are made to do so, he states, "The claim that something real is then measured by these

selected questions is a classic case of reification. It is rather like claiming, as a proof of the existence of God, that he is mentioned in all the books of the Bible" (Lewontin, "The Inferiority Complex," 15).

20. Gould, *The Mismeasure of Man*, 314.

21. Chorover, *From Genesis to Genocide*, 53.

22. ETS researchers, quoted by Rosser, *The SAT Gender Gap*, 5.

23. Ibid., 6.

24. Ibid., 56.

25. Ibid., 13.

26. Ibid.

27. In spring 1987, Brown University students voted on a referendum calling for the school to drop the SAT as an admissions requirement because of its gender, racial, and class bias. About 30 percent of Brown's 5,000 undergraduates voted on the proposal, which was student-initiated. The proposal was narrowly defeated, 777–763 ("Effort to End S.A.T. Testing at Brown U. Is Turned Back," *New York Times*, April 18, 1987, A6).

7. Myth into Method

1. Wigdor and Garner, *Ability Testing*, 1.

2. Arthur R. Jensen, *Bias in Mental Testing* (New York: Free Press, 1980), 42.

3. Ibid., 57.

4. Gardner Murphy, Lois Barclay Murphy, and Theodore M. Newcomb, *Experimental Social Psychology: An Interpretation of Research upon the Socialization of the Individual*, rev. ed. (New York: Harper and Bros., 1937), 53.

5. Some contemporary testers have, however, made a semantic adjustment in describing the comparisons they make between races: rather than calling them "racial" comparisons, they prefer to call them "cultural" comparisons.

6. Robert L. Williams, "Abuses and Misuses in Testing Black Children," ed. Reginald L. Jones, *Black Psychology* (New York: Harper and Row, 1972), 78.

7. David A. Layzer describes the conditions under which this theory applies: "Generally speaking, we should expect to find a normal frequency distribution when the variable part of the measurements in question can be expressed as the sum of many individually small, mutually independent, variable contributions. This is thought to be the case for a number of metric characters of animals such as birth weight in

cattle, staple length of wool, and (perhaps) tentacle length in octopuses" (David A. Layzer, "Science or Superstition? A Physical Scientist Looks at the IQ Controversy," in Block and Dworkin, *The IQ Controversy*, pp. 214–15.)

8. Philip Morrison, "The Bell Shaped Pitfall," in Houts, *The Myth of Measurability*, 86.

9. Ibid., 84.

10. Strenio, *The Testing Trap*, 95.

11. Lawler, *IQ, Heritability and Racism*, 51.

12. Ibid., 49.

13. Ibid., 50.

14. Ibid.

15. Ibid.

16. Williams, "Abuses and Misuses in Testing Black Children," 81.

17. Ibid.

18. Ibid.

19. Herbert Ginsburg, *The Myth of the Deprived Child: Poor Children's Intellect and Education* (Englewood Cliffs, N.J.: Prentice-Hall, 1972), 96.

20. Lawler, *IQ, Heritability and Racism*, 73.

21. This thesis can be traced to Binet's belief that children with lower scores on his intelligence scale had to engage in mental orthopedics or, as he also put it, "learn how to learn," before they could go on to even the most minimal academic pursuits.

22. Lawler, *IQ, Heritability and Racism*, 80.

23. Robert C. Snider, *Back to the Basics?*, a position paper (Washington, D.C.: National Education Association, 1978), 12.

24. Herbert Kohl, *36 Children*; new introduction by Kohl (New York: Plume/New American Library, 1988), viii. Illustrations created by Robert George Jackson III when he was one of the thirty-six children. First published 1967.

25. Ibid., 13.

26. Ibid., 19.

27. Ibid., 25.

28. Ibid., 26.

29. Ibid., 54.

30. Ibid., 38.

31. Ibid., 40.

32. Ibid., 36.

33. Ibid., 57.

34. Ibid., 177.

35. Ibid., 178.
36. Ibid., 205.

8. The Symbiotic Connection

1. George M. Fredrickson, *White Supremacy: A Comparative Study in American and South African History* (New York: Oxford, 1981), 142.
2. Winthrop D. Jordan, *White over Black: American Attitudes Toward the Negro, 1550–1812* (New York: Norton Library, 1977), 436.
3. Quoted in ibid.
4. Quoted in ibid., 438.
5. Quoted in ibid., 438–39.
6. The colonizationists–offering a variant on standard environmentalism—held that blacks had acquired inferior characteristics in this country, which could be overcome if they were returned to Africa. This claim served as the rationale for the colonialists' demand that free blacks be removed immediately to Africa. To lend a semblance of credibility to this demand, they also called for the slaves' removal to Africa—but only at such time as the masters voluntarily freed them. See George M. Fredrickson, *The Black Image in the White Mind: The Debate on Afro-American Character and Destiny, 1817–1914* (New York: Torchbooks, 1972), ch. 1.
7. One researcher is studying the corpus callosum, a structure within the brain, as a source of assumed gender differences in brain functioning (Gina Kolata, *Education Life, New York Times* supplement, August 6, 1989, 25–26). This supposedly new line of research has an antecedent in the work of Robert Bennett Bean, a Virginia physician, who in 1906 published a long, technical article comparing the brains of blacks and whites; it focused in particular on the corpus callosum as the source of presumed black-white, as well as male-female, differences in brain functioning (see Gould, *The Mismeasure of Man*, 77–79).
8. D. Freedman, *Human Sociobiology* (New York: Free Press, 1979). Quoted by Jon Beckwith, "The Political Uses of Sociobiology in the United States and Europe," *Philosophical Forum* 13 (Winter–Spring 1981–82): 314. Beckwith, a Harvard professor of microbiology and molecular genetics, discusses how ultraright groups in England, West Germany, and France used sociobiology to support racist claims. Beckwith, noting the relationship between the use of sociobiology by these groups and its legitimation in the United States, writes: "The result of the barrage of

publicity for sociobiology has been to lend legitimacy to [its] use . . . as an explanatory theory of human culture and social institutions. The legitimacy given to the theory in this country has, in turn, allowed its more extreme use by neofascist and right-wing groups in Europe" (ibid.). Beckwith also stresses that this is not a matter of the misuse of a scientific theory, but rather that "the theory in its very construction" incorporates social values that determine its conclusions (ibid., 319).

9. Quoted by Beckwith, ibid., 318.

10. To support his heritability claim, Jensen relied on Cyril Burt's twin studies. Kamin's exposé of the studies was so devastating—he showed that Burt falsified the correlations between IQ scores of twins—that Jensen was at a loss to defend them. For Kamin's exposé, see his "Separated Identical Twins," in Kamin, *Science and Politics of I.Q.*, 35–47.

11. David A. Layzer, "Science or Superstition? A Physical Scientist Looks at the IQ Controversy," 239.

12. Chorover, *From Genesis to Genocide*, 108.

13. Wigdor and Garner, *Ability Testing*, 93.

14. Otto Klineberg, *Negro Intelligence and Selective Migration*, 14.

15. Ibid., 62.

16. Ibid., 59.

17. Ibid., 16.

18. Arthur R. Jensen, "How Much Can We Boost IQ and Scholastic Achievement?" *Harvard Educational Review* 39 (Winter 1969): 2.

19. Maya Pines, "A Head Start in the Nursery," *Psychology Today* (September 1979): 57.

20. James S. Coleman, et al., *Equality of Educational Opportunity* (Washington, D.C.: U.S. Government Printing Office, 1966).

21. Daniel P. Moynihan, *The Negro Family: The Case for National Action* (Washington, D.C.: U.S. Department of Labor, 1965).

22. For a report on the various studies conducted on Head Start and their effect, see Marshall S. Smith and Joan S. Bissell, "Report Analysis: The Impact of Head Start," *Harvard Educational Review* 40 (Winter 1970): 51–104.

23. Williams, "Abuses and Misuses in Testing Black Children," *Black Psychology*, 80.

24. Ibid.

25. J. McVicker Hunt, *Intelligence and Experience* (New York: Ronald Press, 1961).

26. For an example of Jensen's views when he attributed the alleged verbal deficit to cultural rather than genetic factors, see Jensen, "Social

Class and Verbal Learning," in Martin Deutsch, Irwin Katz, and Arthur R. Jensen, eds., *Social Class, Race and Psychological Development* (New York: Holt, Rinehart and Winston, 1968).

27. C. Bereiter and S. Engelmann, quoted by William Labov, *Language in the Inner City: Studies in the Black English Vernacular* (Philadelphia: University of Pennsylvania Press, 1972), 205.

28. De Lone, *Small Futures,* 134.

29. Joseph White, "Guidelines for Black Psychologists," in Joyce A. Ladner, ed., *The Death of White Sociology* (New York: Vintage, 1973), 256.

30. Labov, *Language in the Inner City,* 232.

31. Labov's work was preceded by pioneer studies of Black English. He writes: "Research on Black English was begun by Black scholars particularly conscious of Black people's African heritage and the resemblance between the language used in the Caribbean and the Black speech forms of the United States. Lorenzo Turner's research on the African elements in Gullah (1949) and Beryl Bailey's description of Jamaican Creole English (1966) provide an excellent foundation for the study of inner-city Black dialects" (Labov, "Recognizing Black English in the Classroom," in John W. Chambers, Jr., ed., *Black English: Educational Equity and the Law* [Ann Arbor, Mich.: Karoma, 1983], 29.)

32. Labov, *Language in the Inner City,* 240.

33. Ibid., 201.

34. Ibid., 229.

35. See J. McVicker Hunt and Girvin E. Kirk, "Social Aspects of Intelligence: Evidence and Issues," in Robert Cancro, ed., *Intelligence: Genetic and Environmental Influences* (New York: Grune and Stratton, 1971). In 1979, by which time he had become known as the "father of Head Start," Hunt also provided a striking example of the symbiotic connection between environmentalism and hereditarianism: "One cannot totally rule out a genetic aspect of race or class differences," he declared. Quoted by Maya Pines in "A Head Start in the Nursery," *Psychology Today* (September 1979): 67.

36. Michael Cole and Jerome S. Bruner, "Cultural Differences and Inferences about Psychological Processes," *American Psychologist* 26 (October 1971): 874.

37. Ibid., 872.

38. Michael Cole et al., *The Cultural Context of Learning and Thinking: An Exploration in Experimental Anthropology* (New York: Basic Books, 1971), 234.

39. Quoted by Labov, "Recognizing Black English in the Classroom," 31.

40. The claims about Black English that could not find a backer in court in 1979 were revived in 1987 in Eleanor Wilson Orr, *Twice as Less: Black English and the Performance of Black Students in Mathematics and Science* (New York: Norton, 1987). According to Orr, a high-school teacher and owner of a private school, black students are ill-equipped for science and mathematics because of a conflict between using Black English and engaging in logical thought. To support this claim, she cited the use by some black students of such expressions as "half more than" for "half less than."

In a refutation of this position, Joseph L. Malone, a professor of linguistics, pointed out that such expressions are "at basis no more mysterious or illogical than standard English expressions such as '(the tank was) more empty (than full)' or '(the prisoner was) found missing (from his cell).' All involve the cognitively inventive combination of apparently incompatible parts to add up to perfectly logical conceptual wholes. Such expressions are conventionalized in standard English, with the ironic consequence that the black student's ingenuity in attempting to encode a semantically tricky relation in an unconventional way may be misunderstood as illogicality." He also noted, "As an instrument of communication and reflection of human genius, black English is in no way inferior to other forms of English. If it anywhere fails to 'add up,' it is only in the blinkered perception of people who themselves fail to understand how human languages really work." Malone, "Linguistic Differences," a letter to The *New York Times Book Review*, November 29, 1987, 38.

41. Gould, *The Mismeasure of Man*, 198.

42. Lawler, *IQ, Heritability and Racism*, 140.

43. Ibid., 163.

44. Karl Marx, "Theses on Feurbach III," in Karl Marx and Friedrich Engels, *The German Ideology*, Part 1, with selections from parts 2 and 3 and supplementary texts, edited by C.J. Arthur (New York: International, 1970), 121.

45. Ginsburg, *The Myth of the Deprived Child*, 100.

46. Ibid., 16.

47. Joyce A. Ladner, "Tomorrow's Tomorrow: The Black Woman," in Ladner, *The Death of White Sociology*, 417–18.

48. The usual description of Banneker as a surveyor of the site for the

nation's capital is incorrect, points out Silvio Bendini, a biographer of Banneker and keeper of rare books at the Smithsonian Institution. Bendini found that Banneker, who used the most sophisticated instruments of his day, maintained a field observatory clock for making the necessary astronomical observations. Reported by William G. Shulz, "Black Scientists in Revolutionary America Struggled to Leave Their Mark," *Los Angeles Times,* April 12, 1984, I–D6.

49. Quoted by Jordan, *White over Black,* 451.

50. Benjamin Banneker, "To Thomas Jefferson," a letter, in Herbert Aptheker, ed., *A Documentary History of the Negro People in the United States* (New York: Citadel, 1951), 23–26.

9. The Testers, South Africa, and the Third World

1. Gustav Jahoda, "Psychology and the Developing Countries: Do They Need Each Other?" *International Social Science Journal* 25, no. 4 (1973): 465.

2. N. Fridja and G. Jahoda, "On the Scope and Methods of Cross-Cultural Research," in D.R. Price Williams, ed., *Cross-Cultural Studies: Selected Readings* (Harmondsworth, Middlesex, England: Penguin, 1969), 29.

3. Arthur G.J. Cryns, "African Intelligence: A Critical Survey of Cross-Cultural Intelligence Research in Africa South of the Sahara," *Journal of Social Psychology* 57 (August 1962): 283–84.

4. The information on the colonial-era tests is from L.E. Andor, ed., *Aptitudes and Abilities of the Black Man in Sub-Saharan Africa: 1784–1963: An Annotated Bibliography* (Johannesburg: National Institute for Personnel Research, 1966); Cryns, "African Intelligence," 283–301; and H.W. Nissen, S. Machover, and Elaine F. Kinder, "A Study of Performance Tests Given to a Group of Native African Negro Children," *British Journal of Psychology,* General Section, 25 (January 1935): 308–55. Andor and Cryns also provide information on craniometry in Africa.

5. The NIPR has published two bibliographies on the studies of "intelligence" in sub-Saharan Africa. The first, L. Andor, ed., *Aptitudes and Abilities of the Black Man in Sub-Saharan Africa: 1784–1963: An Annotated Bibliography,* has entries for about 500 projects. The second, L.E. Andor, ed., *Psychological and Sociological Studies of the Black People of Africa, South of Sahara: 1960–1975: An Annotated Select Bibliography* (Johannesburg: National Institute for Personnel Research, 1982), has a total

of 3,122 entries for authors, African populations tested, and the populations used as control groups.

6. David J.M. Vorster, "Some Recent Cross-Cultural Research of the N.I.P.R.," in John L.M. Dawson and Walter J. Lonner, eds., *Readings in Cross-Cultural Psychology* (Hong Kong: Hong Kong University Press for the International Association for Cross-Cultural Psychology, 1974), 62.

7. Desmond M. Tutu, "Afrikaner Mythology" (review of *The Political Mythology of Apartheid*, by Leonard Thompson), *New York Review of Books*, September 16, 1985, 3.

8. Ibid.

9. Ibid.

10. S. Biesheuval, "Psychological Tests and Their Application to Non-European Peoples," in Price-Williams, *Cross-Cultural Studies: Selected Readings*, 58.

11. S. Biesheuval, "Introduction to the Measurement of Human Performance," in S. Biesheval, ed., *Methods for the Measurement of Psychological Performance: A Handbook of Recommended Methods Based on an IUPS/IBP Working Party*, IBP Handbook No. 10 (London: International Biological Programme; Oxford: Blackwell Scientific Publications 1969), 3.

12. Oliver Tambo, "The Ideology of Racism," *Sechaba* (July 1986): 3. Nelson and Winnie Mandela had been awarded the fifth annual Third World Prize.

13. Vorster, "Some Recent Cross-Cultural Research of the N.I.P.R.," 65.

14. Ibid., 73 and 62.

15. Ibid., 64.

16. Quoted in Andor, *Aptitudes and Abilities of the Black Man in Sub-Saharan Africa: 1784–1963*, 166.

17. S. Biesheuval, "Psychological Tests and Their Application to Non-European Peoples," 68.

18. Michael Cole, John Gay, and Joseph A. Glick, "Some Experimental Studies of Kpelle Quantitative Behavior," in J.W. Berry and P.R. Dasen, eds., *Culture and Cognition: Readings in Cross-Cultural Psychology* (London: Methuen, 1974), 193.

19. Cryns, "African Intelligence," 296. As his use of the phrase "cultural specificity" suggests, Cryns interprets the colonial-era tests from an environmentalist standpoint. This is curious, given his revival of the craniologists' claims.

20. Cole et al., *The Cultural Context of Learning and Thinking*, 215.

21. Michael Cole and Barbara Means, *Comparative Studies of How People Think: An Introduction* (Cambridge: Harvard University Press, 1981), 10.

22. Cole et al., *Learning and Thinking*, 22.

23. S. Biesheuval, foreword to Berry and Dasen, *Culture and Cognition*, xi.

24. Jerome S. Bruner, *The Relevance of Education* (New York: Norton, 1971), 50.

25. Walter Rodney, *How Europe Underdeveloped Africa* (London: Bogle-L'Overture; Dar es Salaam: Tanzania Publishing House, 1972), 30.

26. Ibid., 22.

27. Edward Burnett Tylor, *The Origins of Culture* (Gloucester, Mass.: Peter Smith, 1970), 68. Ten chapters of *Primitive Culture*, first published 1871.

28. Ibid., 111–12.

29. Lucien Lévy-Bruhl, *How Natives Think (Les Fonctions Mentales Dans Les Sociétés Inférieures)*, translated by Lillian A. Clare (London: George Allen and Unwin, 1926), 5.

30. J.W. Berry and P.R. Dasen, "Introduction: History and Method in the Cross-Cultural Study of Cognition," in Berry and Dasen, *Culture and Cognition*, 13.

31. Gould, *The Mismeasure of Man*, 32.

32. Cole et al., *Learning and Thinking*, 232.

33. Michael Cole and Sylvia Scribner, *Culture and Thought: A Psychological Introduction* (New York: Wiley, 1974), 194.

34. The redefinition of Lévy-Bruhl as a cognitive relativist is advanced by C. Scott Littleton, a professor of anthropology, in his introduction to a reprint of *How Natives Think* (Princeton, N.J.: Princeton University Press, 1985).

35. The ease with which an individual who holds one of these positions may shift to the other is illustrated by Bruner. In the same year that he published the article with Cole urging that the cognitive-differences concept replace the cognitive-deficit concept, he also published his revival of the early-arrest thesis, whose unretouched claim of cognitive inequality places it in the cognitive-deficit category.

36. Franz Boas, *The Mind of Primitive Man* (New York: Macmillan, 1911), 122.

37. Ibid., 114.

38. Ibid., 96.

39. Ibid., 248.

40. Lucien Lévy-Bruhl, *The Notebooks on Primitive Mentality*, translated by Peter Rivière (New York: Harper and Row, 1975), 49. The book was first published in France, posthumously, in 1949. Despite the long delay before it was published in this country, and unlike *How Natives Think*, it is out of print.

41. Gould, *The Mismeasure of Man*, 325.

42. Ibid.

43. Lawler, *IQ, Heritability and Racism*, 76, 95.

44. Ibid., 78.

45. The reference is to Desmond Morris, *The Naked Ape* (New York: Dell, 1969).

46. Lawler, *IQ, Heritability and Racism*, 120.

47. Ibid.

48. Ibid., 74.

49. Martin Luther King, Jr., *Where Do We Go from Here: Chaos or Community?* (New York: Bantam, 1968), 86.

50. Amilcar Cabral, "Towards Final Victory," condensed version of an interview recorded at the Khartoum Conference, 1969, in *Revolution in Guinea: Selected Texts by Amilcar Cabral* (New York: Monthly Review Press, 1969), 156–57.

51. Quoted by C. Gerald Fraser, "A New Insight on Nigerian Art," *New York Times*, October 12, 1980, C70. For a many-faceted critique of "primitivism," see Ashley Montagu, ed., *The Concept of the Primitive* (New York: Free Press, 1968).

52. Quoted by John Russell, without further identification, in "Met Pays Homage to Ancient Nigeria," *New York Times*, August 15, 1980, C18.

53. Robert G. Armstrong, *Yoruba Numerals* (Oxford: Oxford University Press for the Nigerian Institute of Social and Economic Research, 1962), 5.

54. Ibid., 7.

55. Claudia Zaslavsky, *Africa Counts: Number and Pattern in African Culture* (Westport, Conn: Lawrence Hill, 1979), 9.

56. Quoted in ibid., 10.

57. W.E.B. Du Bois, *Dusk of Dawn*, 99.

58. Lévy-Bruhl, *How Natives Think*, 1926 ed., 115.

59. Thomas Gladwin, *East is a Big Bird: Navigation and Logic on Puluwat Atoll* (Cambridge: Harvard University Press, 1970), preface.

60. Ibid., 232.

61. Ibid., preface.
62. Ibid.
63. Ibid., 232.
64. Ibid., preface.
65. John Lovell, Jr., "The Social Implications of the Negro Spiritual," *Journal of Negro Education* 8 (October 1939): 642.
66. John Lovell, Jr., *Black Song: The Forge and the Flame* (New York: Macmillan, 1972), 228.
67. Ibid.
68. Ibid.
69. Lovell, "The Social Implications of the Negro Spiritual," 641.
70. Gallagher, *NAACP Report on Minority Testing*, 21. According to the grandfather clause, a male was eligible to vote if his father or grandfather had voted before 1866.
71. W.E.B. Du Bois, *The Souls of Black Folk* (New York: Washington Square Press, 1970), 86. First published 1903.

10. The Risk Factor

1. *Barriers to Excellence: Our Children at Risk* (Boston: National Coalition of Advocates for Students, 1985), viii.
2. *A Nation at Risk: The Imperative for Educational Reform*, National Commission for Excellence in Education (Washington, D.C.: U.S. Department of Education, 1983), 5. In taking the view that children are putting the nation at risk, *A Nation at Risk* extends the pejorative way in which "at risk" is often applied to minority students and students of lower socioeconomic status: that it is somehow their fault that they are at risk of scholastic failure. *Barriers to Excellence,* however, uses the phrase in an accurate way when it points out that the schools and, by extension, the society, put these students at risk.
3. See Lawrence C. Stedman and Carl F. Kaestle, "The Test Score Decline Is Over: Now What?" *Phi Delta Kappan* 67 (November 1985): 206–10.
4. Ibid., 207.
5. Quoted by David Owen, *None of the Above: Behind the Myth of Scholastic Aptitude* (Boston: Houghton Mifflin, 1985), xviii.
6. Ibid.
7. Ibid., xix.

8. Edward B. Fiske, "Lessons: Are Colleges Winning, Or Even Fighting, the Battle to Recruit More Minority Students?" *The New York Times,* April 25, 1990, p. B8. The American Council on Education report, *Status Report on Minorities in Education,* was prepared by Reginald Wilson and Deborah Carter.

9. John Katzman, founder of Princeton Review, a coaching school. Quoted by Owen, *None of the Above,* 138–39.

10. Although Judge Walker found that the SAT discriminates against women, he did not rule against its use for awarding scholarships but instead stipulated that it should not be the only criterion used in the decision-making process. This ruling is wrong in principle: if a criterion is discriminatory, it should be excluded. (After Judge Peckham found that IQ tests are racially discriminatory, he barred their use for placing black children in EMR classes.) With the way left open for discrimination to continue, the New York State Education Department—which had defended in court the SAT-only method of awarding scholarships— added high-school grade-point averages as a criterion, but gave at least twice as much weight to SAT scores. "Though this new system increased the percentage of female winners, girls and minorities are still short-changed," stated FairTest ("Call For End to All SAT Use in NY Scholarships," *FairTest Examiner* 4 [Winter 1989–1990]: 16).

11. *A Nation at Risk,* 28.

12. Florida Commissioner of Education Ralph Turlington, quoted by Thomas H. Fisher in "Florida's Approach to Competency Testing," *Phi Delta Kappan* 59 (May 1978): 601–2.

13. Ibid.

14. *Time,* December 12, 1977, 22.

15. Merle Steven McClung, "Are Competency Testing Programs Fair? Legal?" *Phi Delta Kappan* 59 (February 1978): 398.

16. Gene V. Glass, "Minimum Competence and Incompetence in Florida," *Phi Delta Kappan* 59 (May 1978): 605.

17. Cited by Diana Pullin, "Minimum Competency Testing and the Demand for Accountability," *Phi Delta Kappan* 63 (September 1981): 21.

18. Ibid.

19. Test specialists warn the states that they will look bad not only if their failure rates are "too high," but also if they are "too low," since the latter might be construed to mean they are not pressing vigorously enough for excellence. The "proper" percentages can be arrived at by

adjusting test items after a pilot run. For a discussion on the ways in which the states can have their competency tests constructed to attain the results they desire, see Henry R. Brickell, "Seven Key Notes on Minimum Competency Testing," *Phi Delta Kappan* 59 (May 1978): 589–92.

20. Cited by Linda Darling-Hammond, "Mad-Hatter Tests of Good Teaching," *Education: Winter Survey, New York Times* supplement, January 8, 1984, 57.

21. Arthur E. Wise, "Legislated Learning Revisited," *Phi Delta Kappan* 69 (January 1988): 330.

22. Edward B. Fiske, "Standardized Test Scores: Voodoo Statistics?" *New York Times*, February 17, 1988, B9.

23. Linda Darling-Hammond, quoted by Amy Stuart Wells, "Teacher Tests Assailed as Biased and Vague," *New York Times*, March 16, 1988, B17.

24. See Beverly P. Cole, "The Black Educator: An Endangered Species," *Journal of Negro Education* 55 (Summer 1986): 326–34; and G. Pritchy Smith, *The Effects of Competency Testing on the Supply of Minority Teachers*, report prepared for the National Education Association and the Council of Chief State School Officers, 1987. Smith, who projected that testing along with attrition could reduce the percentage of minority teachers to 5 percent by the year 2000, originally predicted that the percentage would be reduced to this level by 1990. What prevented this from occurring was not a shift in policies but a delay by some states in implementing their testing programs (phone conversation with Smith, April 5, 1990).

25. Thomas R. McDaniel, "The NTE and Teacher Certification," *Phi Delta Kappan* 59 (November 1977): 188. McDaniel is identified as Director of Graduate Education Studies and head of the Division of Social Sciences, Converse College, Spartanburg, S.C.

26. Quoted by Owen in *None of the Above*, 246. The quotation is from an ETS publication, *NTE: Core Battery and Specialty Area Tests* (1983).

27. Wells, "Teacher Tests Assailed as Biased and Vague," B17. The critics of the NTE cited in the article include a panel of test evaluators at the Rand Corporation, the New York Public Interest Group, G. Pritchy Smith, a Columbia Law School committee, and FairTest.

28. Gregory R. Anrig, president of ETS, quoted by Fiske, "Teacher Exam, Often Criticized, to Be Replaced," *New York Times*, October 28, 1988, A1, A17.

29. *Barriers to Excellence: Our Children at Risk*, viii.

30. Ibid., xi.
31. Ibid., 46.
32. Ibid., 11.
33. Ibid., 45–46.
34. Ibid., 47.
35. Ibid.
36. Our comments are based on "The Statement by the President and Governors," *New York Times,* October 1, 1989, sec. 4, p. 22. The statement was issued by the conference of the president and the governors held during the last days of September. (The conference was dubbed the "education summit" by the media.) The statement is filled with the buzzwords associated with testing, e.g., "standards," "performance," "accountability"; it also calls for annual "report cards" on the "progress" of students, schools, states, and the federal government, which will clearly involve comparisons based on test scores. The statement also has an explicit reference to testing, i.e., to student performance on international achievement tests.

Just after the conference was held, the Texas Supreme Court ruled on a matter that was omitted from the summit's agenda: the funding gap between schools in affluent and poor districts. The court held that the state's system for funding public schools is unconstitutional because of "glaring disparities" between rich and poor school districts. See Roberto Suro, "Texas Court Rules Rich-Poor Gap in State School Spending Is Illegal," *New York Times,* October 3, 1989, Al, A15.

37. Tracy Kidder, *Among Schoolchildren* (Boston: Houghton Mifflin, 1989).

38. Teachers attending the annual convention of the National Education Association in July 1983 discussed the attacks then being made on them (8,000 delegates were present). *A Nation at Risk* was cited as an important reason that the onus for the crisis in education was being placed on teachers. "The report doesn't ring true because the blame for the problems with education is put on the teachers. I did not see anything in there about class size and the working conditions of teachers," said Philip Rumore, president of the Buffalo Teachers Federation. Quoted by Gene I. Maeroff, "Teachers Find Politicians' Attention Not At All Welcome," *New York Times,* July 5, 1983, A14.

39. The quotation is from the jacket of *Among Schoolchildren.*

40. Quoted by Lee A. Daniels, "Little Things Add Up to Life," *New York Times Book Review,* September 17, 1989, 46.

41. Kidder, *Among Schoolchildren*, 49.

42. Phyllis Theroux, "One Woman Against the Odds" (review of *Among Schoolchildren*), *New York Times Book Review,* September 17, 1989, 46.

43. Kidder, *Among Schoolchildren*, 28.

44. Ibid., 189.

45. Ibid., 228.

46. Ibid., 7.

47. Ibid., 199.

48. Ibid., 126.

49. Ibid., 52.

50. Vera P. John and Eleanor Leacock, "Transforming the Structure of Failure," in Doxey A. Wilkerson, ed., *Educating All Our Children: An Imperative for Democracy* (Westport, Conn.: Mediax, 1979), 86.

11. One Man's Dream, Another's Nightmare

1. Berkeley Rice, "Brave New World of Intelligence Testing," *Psychology Today* (September 1979): 28–29.

2. Gina Kolata, "Infant I.Q. Tests Found to Predict Scores in School," *New York Times,* April 4, 1989, C1.

3. Deirdre Carmody, "Debate Intensifying on Screening Tests Before Kindergarten," *New York Times,* May 11, 1981, A1, B13.

4. "Not Being Promoted from Kindergarten Is Like the Death of a Parent," *Phi Delta Kappan* 68 (November 1986): 245.

5. Jacqueline Robinson, *The Baby Boards: A Parents' Guide to Preschool and Primary School Entrance Tests* (New York: Prentice-Hall, 1988).

6. This theory is described by the psychometrician Robert J. Sternberg in "Stalking the IQ Quark," *Psychology Today* (September 1979): 42–54. Sternberg discusses an elaborated version of the theory in *The Triarchic Mind: A New Theory of Human Intelligence* (New York: Viking, 1988).

7. For Sternberg's views on analogies as a measure of intelligence, see, e.g., "Stalking the IQ Quark," 45, and *The Triarchic Mind,* 24–25, 64, 115–16.

8. Sternberg, "Stalking the IQ Quark," 49.

9. Howard Gardner, "Beyond the IQ: Education and Human Development," *Harvard Educational Review* 57 (May 1987): 188.

10. Gardner presents his intelligence theory in *Frames of Mind: The Theory of Multiple Intelligences* (New York: Basic Books, 1983).

11. Gardner's expansion of his original number of intelligences is reported by Daniel Goleman, "Rethinking the Value of Intelligence Tests," *Education Life, New York Times* supplement, November 9, 1986, 27.

12. Gardner, "Beyond the IQ," 191.

13. Gardner expresses this view of intelligence tests in *Frames of Mind*, 321.

14. Sternberg makes this point in, e.g., Goleman, "Rethinking the Value of Intelligence Tests," 24.

15. Goleman, ibid., 26.

Bibliography

Ahmann, J. Stanley, and Marvin D. Glock. *Evaluating Pupil Growth: Principles of Tests and Measurements*. 3d ed. Boston: Allyn and Bacon, 1967.

Anastasi, Anne. *Psychological Testing*. 2d ed. New York: Macmillan, 1967.

Andor, L.E., ed. *Aptitudes and Abilities of the Black Man in Sub-Saharan Africa: 1784–1963: An Annotated Bibliography*. Johannesburg: National Institute for Personnel Research, 1966.

————. *Psychological and Sociological Studies of the Black People of Africa South of the Sahara: 1960–1975: An Annotated Select Bibliography*. Johannesburg: National Institute for Personnel Research, 1982.

Applebee, Arthur N., Judith A. Langer, and Ina V. S. Mullis. *Crossroads in American Education*. Based on reports of the National Assessment of Educational Progress. Princeton, N.J.: Educational Testing Service, 1989.

"Aptitude-Test Scores: Grumbling Gets Louder." *U.S. News & World Report* (May 14, 1979): 76–79.

Armstrong, Robert G. *Yoruba Numerals*. Nigerian Social and Economic Studies No. 1. Oxford: Oxford University Press for the Nigerian Institute of Social and Economic Research, 1962.

Asad, Talal, ed. *Anthropology and the Colonial Encounter*. London: Ithaca, 1975.

Bailey, Richard W. "Education and the Law: The King Case in Ann Arbor." In *Black English: Educational Equity and the Law*, edited by John W. Chambers, Jr. Ann Arbor, Mich.: Karoma, 1983.

Banneker, Benjamin. "To Thomas Jefferson," a letter. In *A Documentary History of the Negro People in the United States*, edited by Herbert Aptheker. New York: Citadel, 1951.

Baratz, Joan C. "Language Abilities of Black Americans." In *Comparative Studies of Blacks and Whites in the United States*, edited by Kent S. Miller and Ralph Mason Dreger. New York: Seminar, 1973.

Baratz, Stephen S., and Joan C. Baratz. "Early Childhood Intervention: The Social Science Base of Institutional Racism." *Harvard Educational Review* 40 (Winter 1970): 29–50.

Barriers to Excellence: Our Children at Risk. Introduction by Harold Howe II and Marian Wright Edelman. Boston: National Coalition of Advocates for Students, 1985.

Beckwith, Jon. "The Political Uses of Sociobiology in the United States and Europe." *Philosophical Forum* 13 (Winter–Spring 1981–82): 311–21.

Bennett, Arlene P. "Eugenics as a Vital Part of Institutionalized Racism." *Freedomways* 14 (2nd Quarter 1974): 111–26.

Bennett, Lerone, Jr. *Black Power U.S.A.: The Human Side of Reconstruction, 1867–1877*. Baltimore: Penguin, 1969.

Bereiter, Carl, and Siegfried Engelmann. *Teaching Disadvantaged Children in the Preschool*. Englewood Cliffs, N.J.: Prentice-Hall, 1966.

Bereiter, Carl, et al. "An Academically Oriented Pre-School for Culturally Deprived Children." In *Pre-School Education Today: New Approaches to Teaching Three-, Four-, and Five-Year Olds*, edited by Fred M. Hechinger. Garden City, N.Y.: Doubleday, 1966.

Bernstein, Basil. "Social Class and Linguistic Development: A Theory of Social Learning." In *Education, Economy and Society: A Reader in the Sociology of Education*, edited by A.H. Halsey, Jean Floud, and C. Arnold Anderson. New York: Free Press, 1961.

————. "A Sociolinguistic Approach to Socialization: With Some Reference to Educability." In *Language and Poverty: Perspectives on a Theme*, edited by Frederick Williams. Chicago: Markham, 1971.

Bernstein, Basil, ed. *Class Codes and Control: Applied Studies Toward a Sociology of Language*. Vol. 2. London: Routledge and Kegan Paul, 1973.

Berrueta-Clement, John R., Lawrence J. Schweinhart, W. Steven Barnett, Ann S. Epstein, and David P. Weikart. *Changed Lives: The Effects of the Perry Preschool Program on Youths Through Age 19*. Ypsilanti, Mich.: High/Scope Press, 1984.

Berry, J.W., and P.R. Dasen. "Introduction: History and Method in the Cross-Cultural Study of Cognition." In *Culture and Cognition: Readings in Cross-Cultural Psychology*, edited by J.W. Berry and P.R. Dasen. London: Methuen, 1974.

Bersoff, Donald N. "Legal Constraints on Test Use in the Schools." In *The Uses and Misuses of Tests*, edited by Charles W. Daves. Foreword by Gregory R. Anrig. San Francisco: Jossey-Bass, 1984.

Biesheuval, S. Foreword to *Culture and Cognition: Readings in Cross-Cultural Psychology*, edited by J.W. Berry and P.R. Dasen. London: Methuen, 1974.

————. "Psychological Tests and Their Application to Non-European Peoples." In *Cross Cultural Studies: Selected Readings*, edited by D.R. Price-Williams. Harmondsworth, Middlesex, England: Penguin, 1969.

Biesheuval, S., ed. *Methods for the Measurement of Psychological Performance: A Handbook of Recommended Methods Based on an IUPS/IBP Working Party.* IBP Handbook No. 10. London: International Biological Programme; Oxford: Blackwell Scientific Publications, 1969.

Binder, Frederick W. *The Age of the Common School, 1830–1865.* New York: Wiley, 1974.

Binet, Alfred, and Théodore Simon. *The Development of Intelligence in Children (The Binet-Simon Scale).* Translated by Elizabeth S. Kite. Vineland, N.J.: Vineland Training School; Baltimore: Williams and Wilkins, 1916.

"Black Education 1988." Special issue of *Black Scholar* 19 (November–December 1988).

Block, N.J., and Gerald Dworkin, eds. *The IQ Controversy: Critical Readings.* New York: Pantheon, 1976.

Bloom, Benjamin. *Stability and Change in Human Characteristics.* New York: Wiley, 1964.

Blum, Jeffrey M. *Pseudoscience and Mental Ability: The Origins and Fallacies of the IQ Controversy.* New York: Monthly Review Press, 1978.

Boas, Franz. *The Mind of Primitive Man.* New York: Macmillan, 1911.

———. *Race, Language and Culture.* New York: Macmillan, 1940.

Bowles, Samuel, and Herbert Gintis. *Schooling in Capitalist America: Educational Reform and the Contradictions of Economic Life.* New York: Basic Books, 1976.

Boykin, A. Wade. "Black Psychology and the Research Process: Keeping the Baby but Throwing Out the Bath Water." In *Research Directions of Black Psychologists,* edited by A. Wade Boykin, Anderson J. Franklin, and J. Frank Yates. New York: Russell Sage Foundation, 1980.

Bracey, Gerald W. "Measurement-Driven Instruction: Catchy Phrase, Dangerous Practice." *Phi Delta Kappan* 68 (May 1987): 683–86.

Brickell, Henry R. "Seven Key Notes on Minimum Competency Testing." *Phi Delta Kappan* 59 (May 1978): 589–92.

Brigham, Carl C. "Intelligence Tests of Immigrant Groups." *Psychological Review* 37 (March 1930): 158–65.

———. *A Study of American Intelligence.* Princeton, N.J.: Princeton University Press, 1923.

Brodinsky, Ben. "Back to the Basics: The Movement and Its Meaning." *Phi Delta Kappan* 58 (March 1977): 522–27.

Brodkey, Harold. *Stories in an Almost Classical Mode.* New York: Knopf, 1988.

Brody, Erness Bright, and Nathan Brody. *Intelligence: Nature, Determinants and Consequences.* New York: Academic Press, 1976.

Broudy, Harry S. *The Real World of the Public Schools.* New York: Harcourt Brace Jovanovich, 1972.

Bruner, Jerome S. *The Relevance of Education.* New York: Norton, 1971.

Burnham, Dororthy. "Children of the Slave Community in the United States." *Freedomways* 19 (2nd Quarter 1979): 75–81.

————. "Jensenism: The New Pseudoscience of Racism." *Freedomways* 11 (2nd Quarter 1971): 150–57.

Butler-Omololu, Cynthia, Joseph A. Doster, and Benjamin Lahey. "Some Implications for Intelligence Test Construction and Administration with Children of Different Racial Groups." *Journal of Black Psychology* 10 (February 1984): 63–75.

Cabral, Amilcar. "Towards Final Victory." Condensed version of an interview recorded at the Khartoum Conference, January 1969. In *Revolution in Guinea: Selected Texts by Amilcar Cabral.* New York: Monthly Review Press, 1969.

"Call for End to All SAT Use in NY Scholarships." *FairTest Examiner* 4 (Winter 1989–90): 16.

Caplan, Arthur L., ed. *The Sociobiology Debate: Readings on Ethical and Scientific Issues.* New York: Harper and Row, 1978.

Carroll, Rebecca E. "Can Minorities Survive the Testing Craze?" *The Crisis* 86 (May 1979): 159–61.

Carter, Robert L. "Equal Educational Opportunity for Negroes—Abstraction or Reality." In *With All Deliberate Speed: Civil Rights Theory and Reality,* edited by John H. McCord. Urbana, Ill.: University of Illinois Press, 1969.

Chase, Allan. *The Legacy of Malthus: The Social Costs of the New Scientific Racism.* New York: Knopf, 1977.

Chorover, Stephan L. *From Genesis to Genocide: The Meaning of Human Nature and the Power of Behavior Control.* Cambridge: MIT Press, 1979.

Clark, Kenneth B. *Dark Ghetto: Dilemmas of Social Power.* New York: Harper and Row, 1965.

Clark, Lesley A., and Graeme S. Halford. "Does Cognitive Style Account for Cultural Differences in Scholastic Achievement?" *Journal of Cross-Cultural Psychology* 14 (September 1983): 179–96.

Cole, Beverly P. "The Black Educator: An Endangered Species." *Journal of Negro Education* 55 (Summer 1986): 326–34.

————. "Testing Blacks Out of Education and Employment." *The Crisis* 91 (November 1984): 8–12.

Cole, Michael, and Jerome S. Bruner. "Cultural Differences and Inferences about Psychological Processes." *American Psychologist* 26 (October 1971): 867–76.

Cole, Michael, John Gay, and Joseph A. Glick. "Some Experimental Studies of Kpelle Quantitative Behavior." In *Culture and Cognition: Readings in Cross-Cultural Psychology,* edited by J.W. Berry and P.R. Dasen. London: Methuen, 1974.

Cole, Michael, John Gay, Joseph A. Glick, and Donald W. Sharp. *The Cultural Context of Learning and Thinking: An Exploration in Experimental Anthropology.* New York: Basic Books, 1971.

Cole, Michael, and Barbara Means. *Comparative Studies of How People Think: An Introduction.* Cambridge: Harvard University Press, 1981.

Cole, Michael, and Sylvia Scribner. *Culture and Thought: A Psychological Introduction.* New York: Wiley, 1974.

Coleman, James S. "The Concept of Equality of Educational Opportunity." *Harvard Educational Review* 38 (Winter 1968): 7–22.

Coleman, James S., et al. *Equality of Educational Opportunity.* Washington, D.C.: U.S. Government Printing Office, 1966.

Conant, Levi L. *The Number Concept.* New York: Macmillan, 1889.

Cooper, Constance Carter. "Strategies to Assure Certification and Retention of Black Teachers." *Journal of Negro Education* 55 (Winter 1986): 46–55.

Cronbach, Lee J. "Five Decades of Public Controversy over Mental Testing." *American Psychologist* 30 (January 1975): 1–14.

Cryns, Arthur G.J. "African Intelligence: A Critical Survey of Cross-Cultural Intelligence Research in Africa South of the Sahara." *Journal of Social Psychology* 57 (August 1962): 283–301.

Darling-Hammond, Linda. "Mad Hatter Tests of Good Teaching." *Education: Winter Survey, New York Times* supplement (January 8, 1984): 57.

de Lone, Richard H. *Small Futures: Children, Inequality, and the Limits of Liberal Reform.* For the Carnegie Council on Children. New York: Harcourt Brace Jovanovich, 1979.

Dennis, Wayne. "Goodenough Scores, Art Experience and Modernization." In *Cross-Cultural Studies of Behavior,* edited by Ihsan Al-Issa and Wayne Dennis. New York: Holt, Rinehart and Winston, 1970.

Douglass, Frederick. *The Life and Times of Frederick Douglass.* New York: Collier, 1962. Reprinted from revised edition of 1892.

Du Bois, W.E.B. *Black Reconstruction in America: 1860–1880*. Cleveland: Meridian Books, 1964. First published 1935.

———. *Dusk of Dawn: An Essay Toward an Autobiography of a Race Concept*. With a tribute to Dr. Du Bois by Martin Luther King, Jr. New York: Shocken Books, 1968. First published 1940.

———. *The Souls of Black Folk*. New York: Washington Square Press, 1970. First published 1903.

Eckberg, Douglas Lee. *Intelligence and Race: The Origins and Dimensions of the IQ Controversy*. New York: Praeger, 1979.

Ehrlich, Paul R., and S. Shirley Feldman. *The Race Bomb: Skin Color, Prejudice and Intelligence*. New York: Quadrangle/New York Times, 1977.

Ellison, James. "The Seven Frames of Mind: In His Controversial Theory of Multiple Intelligences, Gardner Challenges Current Definitions and Measurements of Human Potential." Interview with Howard Gardner. *Psychology Today* (June 1984): 21–26.

Evans, Brian, and Bernard Waites. *IQ and Mental Testing: An Unnatural Science and Its Social History*. Atlantic Highlands, N.J.: Humanities Press, 1981.

Eysenck, H.J. *The IQ Argument: Race, Intelligence and Education*. New York: Library Press, 1971.

Eysenck, H.J. vs. Leon Kamin. *The Intelligence Controversy*. New York: Wiley, 1981.

Fallows, James. "The Tests and the 'Brightest': How Fair Are the College Boards?" *Atlantic Monthly* (February 1980): 37–48.

Fine, Benjamin. *The Stranglehold of the I.Q.* Garden City, N.Y.: Doubleday, 1975.

Fisher, Thomas H. "Florida's Approach to Competency Testing." *Phi Delta Kappan* 59 (May 1978): 599–602.

Fiske, Edward B. "America's Test Mania." *Education Life, New York Times* supplement (April 10, 1988): 16–20.

———. "Finding Fault with the Testers." *The New York Times Magazine* (November 18, 1979): 152–62.

Foner, Eric. *Reconstruction: America's Unfinished Revolution 1863–1877*. New York: Harper and Row, 1988.

Franklin, John Hope. *Reconstruction After the Civil War*. Chicago: University of Chicago Press, 1962.

Franklin, Vincent P. "Black Social Scientists and the Mental Testing Movement, 1920–1940." In *Black Psychology*. 2nd ed., edited by Reginald L. Jones. New York: Harper and Row, 1980.

Fredrickson, George M. *The Black Image in the White Mind: The Debate on Afro-American Character and Destiny, 1817–1914*. New York: Torchbooks, 1972.

――――. *White Supremacy: A Comparative Study in American and South African History*. New York: Oxford University Press, 1981.

Freire, Paulo. *The Politics of Education: Culture, Power and Liberation*. Translated by Donaldo Macedo. South Hadley, Mass.: Bergin and Garvey, 1985.

Fridja, N., and Gustav Jahoda. "On The Scope and Methods of Cross-Cultural Research." In *Cross-Cultural Studies: Selected Readings*, edited by D.R. Price-Williams. Harmondsworth, Middlesex, England: Penguin, 1969.

Friedman, Norman L. "Cultural Deprivation: A Commentary on the Sociology of Knowledge." *Journal of Educational Thought* 1 (August 1967): 88–99.

Gallagher, Buell G., ed. *NAACP Report on Minority Testing*. New York: NAACP Special Contribution Fund, 1976.

Gallup, Alec M., and Stanley M. Elam. "The Twentieth Annual Poll of the Public's Attitudes Toward the Public Schools." *Phi Delta Kappan* 70 (September 1988): 33–46.

Garcia, Peter A. "The Impact of National Testing on Ethnic Minorities: With Proposed Solutions." *Journal of Negro Education* 55 (Summer 1986): 347–57.

Gardner, Howard. "Beyond the IQ: Education and Human Development." *Harvard Educational Review* 57 (May 1987): 187–93.

――――. *Frames of Mind: The Theory of Multiple Intelligences*. New York: Basic Books, 1983.

――――. *The Mind's New Science: A History of the Cognitive Revolution*. New York: Basic Books, 1985.

Garth, Thomas Russell. *Race Psychology: A Study of Racial Mental Differences*. New York: McGraw Hill, 1931.

Ginsburg, Herbert. *The Myth of the Deprived Child: Poor Children's Intellect and Education*. Englewood Cliffs, N.J.: Prentice-Hall, 1972.

Ginsburg, Herbert, Jill K. Posner, and Robert L. Russell. "The Development of Mental Addition As a Function of Schooling and Culture." *Journal of Cross-Cultural Psychology* 12 (March 1981): 163–78.

Giroux, Henry A. "Public Philosophy and the Crisis in Education." *Harvard Educational Review* 54 (May 1984): 186–94.

Gladwin, Thomas. "Culture and Logical Process." In *Explorations in*

Cultural Anthropology: Essays in Honor of George Peter Murdock, edited by Ward H. Goodenough. New York: McGraw-Hill, 1964.

————. *East is a Big Bird: Navigation and Logic on Puluwat Atoll.* Cambridge: Harvard University Press, 1970.

Glass, Gene V. "Minimum Competence and Incompetence in Florida." *Phi Delta Kappan* 59 (May 1978): 602–5.

Glass, William. *Schools Without Failure.* New York: Perennial Library, 1969.

Glazer, Nathan. "IQ on Trial." *Commentary* (June 1981): 50–59.

Glazer, Nathan, and Daniel P. Moynihan, eds. *Ethnicity: Theory and Experience.* Cambridge: Harvard University Press, 1975.

Gobineau, Arthur de. *Gobineau: Selected Political Writings,* edited by Michael D. Biddiss. New York: Harper and Row, 1970.

Golden, Mark, and Beverly Birns. "Social Class and Infant Intelligence." In *Origins of Intelligence: Infancy and Early Childhood,* edited by Michael Lewis. New York: Plenum Press, 1976.

Goleman, Daniel. "An Emerging Theory on Blacks' IQ Scores." *Education Life, New York Times* supplement (April 10, 1988): 22–24.

————. "Girls and Math: Is Biology Really Destiny?" *Education Life, New York Times* supplement (August 2, 1987): 42–43.

————. "1,528 Little Geniuses and How They Grew." *Psychology Today* (February 1980): 28–43.

————. "Rethinking the Value of Intelligence Tests." *Education Life, New York Times* supplement (November 9, 1986): 23–27.

Gould, Stephen Jay. Introduction to *Dance of the Tiger,* by Björn Kurtén. New York: Pantheon, 1980.

————. *The Flamingo's Smile: Reflections in Natural History.* New York: Norton, 1985.

————. "Jensen's Last Stand." Review of *Bias in Mental Testing,* by Arthur R. Jensen. *New York Review of Books* (May 1, 1980): 38–44.

————. *The Mismeasure of Man.* New York: Norton, 1981.

————. "Racist Arguments and IQ." In *Race and IQ,* edited by Ashley Montagu. New York: Oxford University Press, 1975.

Greenfield, Patricia Marks. "Comparing Dimensional Categorization in Natural and Artificial Contexts: A Developmental Study Among the Zinacantecos of Mexico." *Journal of Social Psychology* 93 (August 1974): 157–71.

Gregoire, Henri. *An Enquiry Concerning the Intellectual and Moral Faculties and Literature of Negroes: Followed with an Account of the Life and Works of*

Fifteen Negroes and Mulattoes Distinguished in Science, Literature and the Arts. Translated by D.B. Warden. College Park, Md.: McGrath, 1967. First published 1810.

Grigsby, J., Eugene. "Ba Kuba Art Exhibited at the Universal and International Exposition of Bruxelles 1958." In *Africa Seen by American Negro Scholars.* New York: The American Society of African Culture, 1963.

Guthrie, Robert V. *Even the Rat Was White: A Historical View of Psychology.* New York: Harper and Row, 1976.

Gutman, Herbert. *The Black Family in Slavery and Freedom, 1750–1925.* New York: Pantheon, 1976.

Halliburton, Warren J. "The Fallacy of Testing for Minorities." *Freedomways* 16 (1st Quarter 1976): 34–38.

Handlin, Oscar. *Race and Nationality in American Life.* New York: Little, Brown, 1957.

Harding, Thomas G., David Kaplan, Marshall D. Sahlins, and Elman R. Service. *Evolution and Culture,* edited by Marshall D. Sahlins and Elmer R. Service. Ann Arbor: University of Michigan Press, 1960.

Harris, Adrienne. "Are Brains Genetic?" Review of *The Intelligence Controversy,* H.J. Eysenck vs. Leon Kamin. *New York Times Book Review* (May 3, 1981): 11, 22.

Harris, Dale B. *Children's Drawings as Measures of Intellectual Maturity: A Revision and Extension of the Goodenough Draw-a-Man Test.* New York: Harcourt Brace Jovanovich, 1963.

Hart, Gary K. "The California Pupil Proficiency Law as Viewed by Its Author." *Phi Delta Kappan* 59 (May 1978): 592–95.

Herrnstein, Richard J. "I.Q." *Atlantic Monthly* (September 1971): 43–64.

———. *I.Q. in the Meritocracy.* Boston: Atlantic Monthly Press and Little, Brown, 1973.

———. "I.Q. Testing and the Media." *Atlantic Monthly* (August 1982): 68–74.

Herskovits, Melville J. *Cultural Relativism: Perspectives in Cultural Pluralism.* Edited by Frances Herskovits. New York: Vintage, 1973.

———. *Franz Boas: The Science of Man in the Making.* New York: Scribner's, 1953.

———. *The Myth of the Negro Past.* Boston: Beacon, 1958. First published 1941.

Hilliard, Asa G., III. "IQ and the Courts: Larry P. vs. Wilson Riles and PASE vs. Hannon." *Journal of Black Psychology* 10 (August 1983): 1–18.

Hoffmann, Banesh. *The Tyranny of Testing*. New York: Crowell-Collier, 1962.

Houts, Paul L. "A Conversation with Banesh Hoffmann." In *The Myth of Measurability*, edited by Paul L. Houts. New York: Hart, 1977.

Hunt, J. McVicker. "Has Compensatory Education Failed? Has It Been Attempted?" *Harvard Educational Review* 39 (Spring 1969): 278–300.

———. *Intelligence and Experience*. New York: Ronald Press, 1961.

Hunt, J. McVicker, and Girvin E. Kirk. "Social Aspects of Intelligence: Evidence and Issues." In *Intelligence: Genetic and Environmental Influences*, edited by Robert Cancro. New York: Grune and Stratton, 1971.

Hunt, Morton. *The Universe Within: A New Science Explores the Human Mind*. New York: Simon and Schuster, 1982.

Imperiled Generation: Saving Urban Schools. A Carnegie Foundation Special Report. Princeton, N.J.: Carnegie Foundation for the Advancement of Teaching, 1988.

Jahoda, Gustav. "Presidential Address: Applying Cross-Cultural Psychology to the Third World." In *Applied Cross-Cultural Psychology*, edited by J.W. Berry and W.J. Lonner. Amsterdam: Swets and Zeitlinger for the International Association for Cross-Cultural Psychology, 1975.

———. "Psychology and the Developing Countries: Do They Need Each Other?" *International Social Science Journal* 25, no. 4 (1973): 461–74.

———. Foreword to *Readings in Cross-Cultural Psychology*, edited by John L.M. Dawson and Walter J. Lonner. Hong Kong: Hong Kong University Press for the International Association for Cross-Cultural Psychology, 1971.

Jaynes, Gerald D., and Robin M. Williams, Jr., eds. *A Common Destiny: Blacks and American Society*. Committee on the Status of Black Americans, Commission on Behavioral and Social Sciences and Education, National Research Council. Washington, D.C.: National Academy Press, 1989.

Jencks, Christopher, et al. *Inequality: A Reassessment of the Effect of Family and Schooling in America*. New York: Harper Colophon Books, 1972.

Jensen, Arthur R. *Bias in Mental Testing*. New York: Free Press, 1980.

———. "How Much Can We Boost IQ and Scholastic Achievement?" *Harvard Educational Review* 39 (Winter 1969): 1–123.

———. "Social Class and Verbal Learning." In *Social Class, Race, and Psychological Development*, edited by Martin Deutsch, Irwin Katz, and Arthur R. Jensen. New York: Holt, Rinehart and Winston, 1968.

John, Vera P., and Eleanor Leacock. "Transforming the Structure of Failure. In *Educating All Our Children: An Imperative for Democracy*, edited by Doxey A. Wilkerson. Westport, Conn.: Mediax, 1979.

Jones, Nicholas Blurton, and Melvin J. Konner. "!Kung Knowledge of Animal Behavior." In *Kalahari Hunter-Gatherers: Studies of the !Kung San and Their Neighbors*, edited by Richard B. Lee and Irven De Vore. Cambridge: Harvard University Press, 1976.

Jones, Rhett S. "Proving Blacks Inferior: The Sociology of Knowledge." In *The Death of White Sociology*, edited by Joyce A. Ladner. New York: Vintage, 1973.

Jones, Syl. "William Shockley: A Candid Conversation with the Nobel Prize Winner—in Physics—about His Theories on Black Inferiority and His Donation of Sperm for a 'Super Baby.'" *Playboy*, August 1980: 69–102.

Jordan, Winthrop D. *White over Black: American Attitudes Toward the Negro, 1550–1812*. New York: Norton Library, 1977.

Kamin, Leon J. *The Science and Politics of IQ*. Potomac, Md.: Lawrence Erlbaum, 1974.

Katz, Michael B. *Class, Bureaucracy and Schools: The Illusion of Educational Change in America*. New York: Praeger, 1971.

Katz, Michael B., ed. *School Reform: Past and Present*. Boston: Little, Brown, 1971.

Keesing, Felix M. *Cultural Anthropology: The Science of Custom*. New York: Holt, Rinehart and Winston, 1958.

Kellaghan, Thomas. "Abstraction and Classification in African Children." *International Journal of Psychology* 3, no. 2 (1968): 115–20.

Kerner, Otto, et al. *Report of the National Advisory Commission on Civil Disorders*. New York: Dutton, 1968.

The Kerner Report Updated: Report of the 1988 Commission on the Cities—Race and Poverty in the United States Today. National Conference: "The Kerner Report Twenty Years Later." Fred R. Harris and Roger Wilkins, co-chairs.

Kidder, Tracy. *Among Schoolchildren*. Boston: Houghton Mifflin, 1989.

King, Martin Luther, Jr. *Where Do We Go from Here: Chaos or Community?* New York: Bantam, 1968.

Kitcher, Philip. *Vaulting Ambition: Sociobiology and the Quest for Human Nature*. Cambridge: MIT Press, 1985.

Klineberg, Otto. *Negro Intelligence and Selective Migration*. New York: Columbia University Press, 1935.

————. *Race Differences.* New York: Harper and Brothers, 1935.

Kohl, Herbert. *36 Children.* With a new introduction by the author. New York: Plume/New American Library, 1988. Illustrated by Robert George Jackson III. First published in 1967.

Kolata, Gina. "Mind Blowing? Brains May Differ by Sex, but No One Is Sure What It Means." *Education Life, New York Times* supplement (August 6, 1989): 25–26.

Konner, Melvin. *The Tangled Wing: Biological Constraints on the Human Spirit.* New York: Holt, Rinehart and Winston, 1982.

Kozol, Jonathan. *Death at an Early Age: The Destruction of the Hearts and Minds of Negro Children in the Boston Public Schools.* New York: Houghton Mifflin, 1967.

Krippner, Stanley. "Race, Intelligence, and Segregation: The Misuse of Scientific Data." In *White Racism: Its History, Pathology and Practice,* edited by Barry N. Schwartz and Robert Disch. New York: Dell, 1970.

Laboratory of Comparative Human Cognition, University of California at San Diego. "Cross Cultural Psychology's Challenges to Our Ideas of Children and Development." *American Psychologist* 34 (October 1979): 827–33.

Labov, William. *Language in the Inner City: Studies in the Black English Vernacular.* Philadelphia: University of Pennsylvania Press, 1972.

————. "Recognizing Black English in the Classroom." In *Black English: Educational Equity and the Law,* edited by John W. Chambers, Jr. Ann Arbor, Mich.: Karoma, 1983.

Ladner, Joyce A. "Tomorrow's Tomorrow: The Black Woman." In *The Death of White Sociology,* edited by Joyce A. Ladner. New York: Vintage, 1973.

Lawler, James M. *IQ, Heritability and Racism.* New York: International, 1978.

Layzer, David A. "Science or Superstitition? A Physical Scientist Looks at the IQ Controversy." In *The IQ Controversy: Critical Readings,* edited by N.J. Block and Gerald Dworkin. New York: Pantheon, 1976.

Lévi-Strauss, Claude. *The Savage Mind.* Chicago: University of Chicago Press, 1966.

Lévy-Bruhl, Lucien. *How Natives Think (Les Fonctions Mentales Dans Les Sociétés Inférieures).* Translated by Lillian A. Clare. London: Allen and Unwin, 1926.

————. *The Notebooks on Primitive Mentality.* Translated by Peter Rivière. New York: Harper and Row, 1975. First published in France in 1949.

————. *Primitive Mentality.* Translated by Lillian A. Clare. London: Allen and Unwin, 1923.

Lewis, Donald Marion. "Testing and Its Legal Limits—The Florida Decision." *Today's Education* 68 (November–December 1979): 25–28.

Lewontin, R.C. "The Inferiority Complex." Review of *The Mismeasure of Man,* by Stephen Jay Gould. *The New York Review of Books* (October 22, 1981): 12–16.

Lewontin, R.C., Steven Rose, and Leon J. Kamin. *Not in Our Genes: Biology, Ideology, and Human Nature.* New York: Pantheon, 1984.

Lippmann, Walter. "The Lippmann-Terman Debate." In *The IQ Controversy: Critical Readings,* edited by N.J. Block and Gerald Dworkin. New York: Pantheon, 1976.

Littleton, C. Scott. "Lucien Lévy-Bruhl and the Concept of Cognitive Relativity." New introduction to *How Natives Think,* by Lucien Lévy-Bruhl. Translated by Lillian A. Clare. Princeton, N.J.: Princeton University Press, 1985.

Lorentan, Joseph O., and Shelley Umans. *Teaching the Disadvantaged: New Curriculum Approaches.* New York: Teachers College Press, 1966.

Lovell, John, Jr. *Black Song: The Forge and the Flame.* New York: Macmillan, 1972.

————. "The Social Implications of the Negro Spiritual." *Journal of Negro Education* 8 (October 1939): 634–43.

MacKenzie, Brian. "Explaining Race Differences in IQ: The Logic, the Methodology, and the Evidence." *American Psychologist,* 39 (November 1984): 1214–33.

Malone, Joseph L. "Linguistic Differences," a letter. *New York Times Book Review* (November 29, 1987): 38.

Marshack, Alexander. "A Lunar-Solar Year Calendar Stick from North America." *American Antiquity* 50 (January 1985): 27–51.

Marshall, Paule. "From the Poets in the Kitchen: The Making of a Writer." *New York Times Book Review* (January 9, 1983).

Marx, Karl. "Theses on Feuerbach III." In *Karl Marx and Friedrich Engels, The German Ideology,* Part 1, with selections from parts 2 and 3 and supplementary text. Edited by C.J. Arthur. New York: International, 1970.

McClung, Merle Steven. "Are Competency Testing Programs Fair? Legal?" *Phi Delta Kappan* 59 (February 1978): 397–400.

McDaniel, Thomas R. "The NTE and Teacher Certification." *Phi Delta Kappan* 59 (November 1977): 186–88.

Mead, Margaret. *Coming of Age in Samoa: A Psychological Study of Primitive Youth for Western Civilization.* New York: Morrow, 1955. First published 1928.

Mehler, Barry. "The New Eugenics: Academic Racism in the U.S. Today." *Science for the People* 15 (May–June 1983): 18–23.

Meier, Deborah. "Why Reading Tests Don't Test Reading." *Dissent* 28 (Fall 1981): 457–66.

Mercer, Jane R., and Wayne Curtis Brown. "Racial Differences in I.Q.: Fact or Artifact?" In *The Fallacy of I.Q.,* edited by Carl Senna. New York: The Third Press, 1973.

Mitchell, Jacquelyn. "Reflections of a Black Social Scientist: Some Struggles, Some Doubts, Some Hopes." *Harvard Educational Review* 52 (February 1982): 27–44.

Montagu, Ashley. *The Idea of Race.* Lincoln, Neb.: University of Nebraska Press, 1965.

———. *Statement on Race.* New York: Henry Schuman, 1951.

Montagu, Ashley, ed. *The Concept of the Primitive.* New York: Free Press, 1968.

———. *Frontiers of Anthropology.* Introduction and notes by Montagu. New York: G.P. Putnam's Sons, 1974.

Montagu, M.F. Ashley. "Intelligence of Northern Negroes and Southern Whites in the First World War." *American Journal of Psychology* 58 (April 1945): 161–88.

Morris, Desmond. *The Naked Ape.* New York: Dell, 1969.

Morrison, Philip. "The Bell Shaped Pitfall." In *The Myth of Measurability,* edited by Paul L. Houts. New York: Hart, 1977.

Moynihan, Daniel P. *The Negro Family: The Case for National Action.* Washington, D.C.: U.S. Department of Labor, 1965.

Muffler, John P. "Education and the Separate but Equal Doctrine." *Black Scholar* 17 (May–June 1986): 35–41.

Murphy, Gardner, Lois Barclay Murphy, and Theodore M. Newcomb. *Experimental Social Psychology: An Interpretation of Research upon the Socialization of the Individual.* Rev. ed. New York: Harper and Bros., 1937.

Murphy, Lois Barclay, and Gardner Murphy. "Perspectives in Cross-Cultural Research." *Journal of Cross-Cultural Psychology* 1 (Spring 1970): 1–4.

A Nation at Risk: The Imperative for Educational Reform. National Commission on Excellence in Education. Washington, D.C.: U.S. Department of Education, 1983.

Neill, D. Monty, and Noe J. Medina. "Standardized Testing: Harmful to Educational Health." *Phi Delta Kappan* 70 (May 1989): 688–97.

Nimmicht, Glen P., et al. *Beyond "Compensatory Education: A New Approach to Educating Children."* San Francisco: Far West Laboratory for Educational Research and Development, 1973.

Nissen, H.W., S. Machover, and Elaine F. Kinder. "A Study of Performance Tests Given to a Group of Native African Negro Children." *British Journal of Psychology*, General Section, 25 (January 1935): 308–55.

Oakes, Jeannie. *Keeping Track: How Schools Structure Inequality.* New Haven: Yale University Press, 1985.

Ogbu, John U. "Minority Education and Caste: The American System in Cross-Cultural Perspective." *The Crisis* 86 (January 1979): 17–21.

Ong, Walter J. *Orality and Literacy: The Technologizing of the Word.* London: Methuen, 1982.

Orr, Eleanor Wilson. *Twice as Less: Black English and the Performance of Black Students in Mathematics and Science.* New York: Norton, 1987.

Owen, David. "The Last Days of ETS." *Harper's* (May 1983): 21–37.

————. *None of the Above: Behind the Myth of Scholastic Aptitude.* Boston: Houghton Mifflin, 1985.

Padilla, Amado M., and Blas M. Garza. "I.Q. Tests: A Case of Cultural Myopia." In *The Myth of Measurability*, edited by Paul L. Houts. New York: Hart, 1977.

Paynter, Edward L. "Value Premises in Race Research: The Evolution of Environmentalism." In *Race, Change, and Urban Society*, edited by Peter Orleans and William Russell Ellis, Jr. Beverly Hills, Calif.: Sage Publications, 1971.

Persell, Caroline Hodges. *Education and Inequality: A Theoretical and Empirical Synthesis.* New York: Free Press, 1977.

————. "Genetic and Cultural Deficit Theories: Two Sides of the Same Racist Coin." *Journal of Black Studies* 12 (September 1981): 19–37.

Peterson, Joseph. *Early Conceptions and Tests of Intelligence.* Yonkers-On-Hudson, N.Y.: World Book Co., 1925.

Piaget, Jean. *The Psychology of Intelligence.* Translated by M. Piercy and D.E. Berlynel. London: Routledge and Kegan Paul, 1947.

Pines, Maya. "A Head Start in the Nursery." *Psychology Today* (September 1979): 56–68.

Pipho, Chris. "Minimum Competency Testing in 1978: A Look at State Standards." *Phi Delta Kappan* 59 (May 1978): 585–88.

Popham, W. James. "The Merits of Measurement-Driven Instruction." *Phi Delta Kappan* 68 (May 1987): 679–82.

Popham, W. James, and Elaine Lindheim. "Implications of a Landmark Ruling on Florida's Minimum Competency Test." *Phi Delta Kappan* 63 (September 1981): 18–20.

Porteus, Stanley D. *The Psychology of a Primitive People: A Study of the Australian Aborigine.* Freeport, N.Y.: Books for Libraries Press, 1972. First published 1931.

Principal, editors of. "The Score Against IQ: A Look at Some Test Items." In *The Myth of Measurability,* edited by Paul L. Houts. New York: Hart, 1977.

Pullin, Diana. "Minimum Competency Testing and the Demand for Accountability." *Phi Delta Kappan* 63 (September 1981): 20–22.

Rainwater, Lee, and William L. Yancey. *The Moynihan Report and the Politics of Controversy.* Cambridge: MIT Press, 1967.

Ravitch, Diane. "Value of Standardized Tests in Indicating How Well Students Are Learning." In *The Uses and Misuses of Tests,* edited by Charles W. Daves. San Francisco: Jossey-Bass, 1984.

Rebelsky, Freda, and Patricia A. Daniel. "Cross Cultural Studies of Infant Intelligence." In *Origins of Intelligence: Infancy and Early Childhood,* edited by Michael Lewis. New York: Plenum Press, 1976.

Rice, Berkeley. "Brave New World of Intelligence Testing." *Psychology Today* (September 1979): 26–41.

———. "Going for the Gifted Gold." *Psychology Today* (February 1980).

Riessman, Frank. *The Culturally Deprived Child.* New York: Harper and Row, 1962.

Rist, Ray C. "Student Social Class and Teacher Expectations: The Self-Fulfilling Prophecy in Ghetto Education." *Harvard Educational Review* 40 (August 1970): 411–51.

Rivers, W.H.R. "Vision." In *Reports of the Cambridge Anthropological Expedition to Torres Straits,* edited by A.C. Haddon. Vol. 1 New York: Johnson Reprint, 1971. First published 1901.

Robinson, Jacqueline. *The Baby Boards: A Parents' Guide to Preschool and Primary School Entrance Tests.* New York: Prentice-Hall, 1988.

Rodney, Walter. *How Europe Underdeveloped Africa.* London: Bogle-L'Overture; Dar es Salaam: Tanzania Publishing House, 1972.

Rose, Steven, and Hilary Rose. "Less than Human Nature: Biology and the New Right." *Race and Class* 37 (Winter 1986): 47–66.

Rosenthal, Robert. "The Pygmalion Effect Lives." *Psychology Today* (September 1973): 56–63.

Rosenthal, Robert, and Lenore Jacobson. *Pygmalion in the Classroom: Teacher Expectation and Pupils' Intellectual Development.* New York: Holt, Rinehart and Winston, 1968.

Rosser, Phyllis. *The SAT Gender Gap: Identifying the Causes.* Washington, D.C.: Center for Women Policy Studies, 1989.

Rothstein, Stanley William. "The Abandonment of the Public Schools." *The Crisis* 86 (January 1979): 27–31.

Schwartz, Judah L. "A Is to B as C Is to Anything at All: The Illogic of IQ Tests." In *The Myth of Measurability,* edited by Paul L. Houts. New York: Hart, 1977.

Schwebel, Milton. *Who Can Be Educated?* New York: Grove, 1988.

Scribner, Sylvia, and Michael Cole. *The Psychology of Literacy.* Cambridge: Harvard University Press, 1981.

Sharp, Donald, Michael Cole, and Charles Lave. *Education and Cognitive Development: The Evidence from Experimental Research.* Commentary by Herbert Ginsburg, Ann L. Brown, and Lucia A. French. Reply by Michael Cole. Monographs of the Society for Research in Child Development, serial no. 178, vol. 44, nos. 1–2. Chicago: University of Chicago Press, 1979.

Shor, Ira. *Culture Wars: Schools and Society in the Conservative Restoration 1969–1984.* Boston: Routledge and Kegan Paul, 1986.

Shuey, Audrey M. *The Testing of Negro Intelligence.* 2d ed. New York: Social Science Press, 1966.

Silberman, Charles E. *Crisis in Black and White.* New York: Random House, 1964.

Smith, G. Pritchy. *The Effects of Competency Testing on the Supply of Minority Teachers.* Report prepared for the National Education Association and the Council of Chief State School Officers, 1987.

———. *Increasing the Number of Minority Teachers: Recommendations for a Call to Action.* Paper prepared for the Quality Education for Minorities Project, Massachusetts Institute of Technology, 1989.

Smith, Marshall S., and Joan S. Bissell. "Report Analysis: The Impact of Head Start." *Harvard Educational Review* 40 (Winter 1970): 51–104.

Smitherman, Geneva. *Talkin and Testifyin: The Language of Black America.* Boston: Houghton Mifflin, 1977.

Snider, Robert C. *Back to the Basics?* A position paper. Washington, D.C.: National Education Association, 1978.

Snyderman, Mark, and Richard J. Herrnstein. "Intelligence Tests and the Immigration Act of 1924." *American Psychologist* 38 (September 1983): 986–95.

Spearman, Charles. *The Abilities of Man*. New York: Macmillan, 1927.

Stanton, William. *The Leopard's Spots: Scientific Attitudes Toward Race in America 1815–59*. Chicago: University of Chicago Press, 1960.

Stedman, Lawrence C., and Carl F. Kaestle. "The Test Score Decline Is Over: Now What?" *Phi Delta Kappan* 67 (November 1985): 206–10.

Steinberg, Stephen. *The Ethnic Myth: Race, Ethnicity, and Class in America*. New York: Atheneum, 1981.

Stern, Bernhard J. *Lewis Henry Morgan: Social Evolutionist*. Chicago: University of Chicago Press, 1931.

Sternberg, Robert J. "Stalking the IQ Quark." *Psychology Today* (September 1979): 42–54.

———. "Testing Intelligence Without I.Q. Tests." *Phi Delta Kappan* 65 (June 1984): 694–700.

———. *The Triarchic Mind: A New Theory of Human Intelligence*. New York: Viking, 1988.

Strenio, Andrew J., Jr. *The Testing Trap*. New York: Rawson, Wade: 1981.

Sullivan, Otha Richard. "Who's Testing Black Children and Youth in the Public Schools?" *Freedomways* 21 (2nd Quarter 1981): 114–18.

Taba, Hilda. "Cultural Deprivation as a Factor in School Learning." *Merrill-Palmer Quarterly* 10 (April 1964): 147–60.

Tambo, Oliver. "The Ideology of Racism." *Sechaba* (July 1986): 2–8.

Terman, Lewis M. *The Intelligence of School Children: How Children Differ in Ability, the Use of Mental Tests in School Grading and the Proper Education of Exceptional Children*. Boston: Houghton Mifflin, 1919.

———. "The Lippmann-Terman Debate." In *The IQ Controversy: Critical Readings*, edited by N.J. Block and Gerald Dworkin. New York: Pantheon, 1976.

———. *The Measurement of Intelligence: An Explanation of and a Complete Guide for the Use of the Stanford Revision and Extension of the Binet-Simon Intelligence Scale*. Boston: Houghton-Mifflin, 1916.

Terman, Lewis M., and Maud A. Merrill. *Measuring Intelligence: A Guide to the Administration of the New Revised Stanford-Binet Tests of Intelligence*. Boston: Houghton Mifflin, 1937.

"Testing African American Students." *Negro Educational Review* 38 (April–June 1987): special issue.

Theroux, Phyllis. "One Woman Against the Odds." Review of *Among*

Schoolchildren, by Tracy Kidder. *New York Times Book Review* (September 17, 1989), 1, 46.

Time for Assertive Action: School Strategies for Promoting the Educational Success of At-Risk Children. Report of the Commissioner's Task Force on the Education of Children and Youth-at-Risk. Commissioned by New York State Education Commissioner Thomas Sobol. Albany, N.Y.: State Education Department/University of the State of New York, 1988.

Tractenberg, Paul L. "Legal Issues in the Testing of School Personnel." *Phi Delta Kappan* 57 (May 1976): 602–5.

Tuddenham, Read D. "The Nature and Measurement of Intelligence." In *Psychology in the Making: Histories of Selected Research Problems*, edited by Leo Postman. New York: Knopf, 1962.

Tutu, Desmond M. "Afrikaner Mythology." Review of *The Political Mythology of Apartheid*, by Leonard Thompson. In *New York Review of Books* (September 16, 1985): 3–4.

Tyack, David. *The One Best System: A History of American Urban Education.* Cambridge: Harvard University Press, 1974.

Tyack, David, and Elisabeth Hansot. "Hard Times, Then and Now: Public Schools in the 1930s and 1980s." *Harvard Educational Review* 54 (February 1984): 33–66.

Tylor, Edward Burnett. *The Origins of Culture.* Chap. 1–10 of *Primitive Culture.* Gloucester, Mass.: Peter Smith, 1970. *Primitive Culture* was first published in 1871.

Valentine, Charles A. "Deficit, Difference, and Bicultural Models of Afro-American Behavior." *Harvard Educational Review* 41 (May 1971): 137–51.

Vernon, Philip E. *Intelligence: Heredity and Environment.* San Francisco: Freeman, 1979.

Vorster, David J. M. "Some Recent Cross-Cultural Research of the N.I.P. R." In *Readings in Cross-Cultural Psychology*, edited by John L.M. Dawson and Walter J. Lonner. Hong Kong: Hong Kong University Press for the International Association for Cross-Cultural Psychology, 1974.

Weaver, Edward K. "The New Literature on Education of the Black Child." In *What Black Educators Are Saying*, edited by Nathan Wright, Jr. New York: Hawthorn Books, 1970.

What Works: Research About Teaching and Learning. Washington, D.C.: U.S. Department of Education, 1986.

Whimbey, Arthur, with Linda Shaw Whimbey. *Intelligence Can Be Taught.* New York: Dutton, 1980.

White, Joseph. "Guidelines for Black Psychologists." In *The Death of White Sociology,* edited by Joyce A. Ladner. New York: Vintage, 1973.

Whitten, Norman E., Jr., and John F. Szwed, eds. *Afro-American Anthropology: Contemporary Perspectives.* New York: Free Press, 1970.

Wigdor, Alexandra K., and Wendell R. Garner, eds. *Ability Testing: Uses, Consequences, and Controversies.* Part 1. Washington, D.C.: National Academy Press, 1982.

Wilkerson, Doxey A., ed. Editor's introduction. *Educating All Our Children: An Imperative for Democracy.* Westport, Conn.: Mediax, 1979.

————. "Standardizing Children." *Freedomways* 17 (4th Quarter 1977): 197–201.

Williams, Robert L. "Abuses and Misuses in Testing Black Children." In *Black Psychology,* edited by Reginald L. Jones. New York: Harper and Row, 1972.

Wilson, Edward O. *Sociobiology: The New Synthesis.* Cambridge: Harvard University Press, 1975.

Wise, Arthur E. *Legislated Learning: The Bureaucratization of the American Classroom.* Berkeley, Calif.: University of California Press, 1979.

————. "Legislated Learning Revisited." *Phi Delta Kappan* 69 (January 1988): 328–33.

————. "Minimum Competency Testing: Another Case of Hyper-Rationalization." *Phi Delta Kappan* 59 (May 1978): 596–98.

Witty, Elaine P. "Testing Teacher Performance." *Journal of Negro Education* 55 (Summer 1986): 358–67.

Wober, Mallory. "A Crossroads for Cross-Cultural Psychology." *IACCP Cross-Cultural Psychology Newsletter* 11 (June 1977): 2–4.

Wolf, Theta H. *Alfred Binet.* Chicago: University of Chicago Press, 1973.

Yerkes, Robert M., ed. "Psychological Examining in the United States Army," *Memoirs of the National Academy of Sciences,* vol. 15. Washington, D.C.: U.S. Government Printing Office, 1921.

Young, Michael. *The Rise of the Meritocracy, 1870–2033: An Essay on Education and Equality.* London: Thames and Hudson, 1958.

Zaslavsky, Claudia. *Africa Counts: Number and Pattern in African Culture.* Westport, Conn.: Lawrence Hill, 1979.

Index